Editor

Eric Migliaccio

Managing Editor

Ina Massler Levin, M.A.

Illustrator

Mark Mason

Cover Artist

Marilyn Goldberg

Art Production Manager

Kevin Barnes

Art Coordinator

Renée Christine Yates

Imaging

Rosa C. See

Publisher

Mary D. Smith, M.S. Ed.

READY•TO•GO LESSONS

Reading & Writing

Grade 4

✔ Organizational Patterns
✔ Literary Language
✔ Fables, Myths, & Fairy Tales
✔ Making Predictions
✔ Character Development
...and more!

Ideal for Substitute Teachers

Author

Jessica M. Dubin Kissel, M. A.

Teacher Created Resources, Inc.

6421 Industry Way

Westminster, CA 92683

www.teachercreated.com

ISBN-1-4206-8033-1

©2006 Teacher Created Resources, Inc.

Made in U.S.A.

Teacher Created Resources

Table of Contents

Introduction

The Concept

Every teacher needs and deserves more time. And excellent teachers know that to create excellent lesson plans, it takes time. The lessons in *Ready to Go, Grade 4* are completed lesson plans written specifically for fourth-grade language-arts teachers to use throughout the year. They will come in handy for teachers who are short on time, need complete substitute lesson plans, or just want a lesson to incorporate into their units—specifically, a lesson that they did not have to take the time to design!

Each lesson is broken down into a reading and writing component. The reading and writing sections of each lesson were designed to enhance one another, but most of them can be taught separately, as well. Each lesson can be easily altered to match different teaching and learning styles.

An Overview

- ✔ The lessons provided in this book use clearly-written and simply-designed teaching frameworks that are easy to follow.

- ✔ Depending on the ability of the students, the length of time it will take to complete the lessons will vary.

- ✔ Most materials that are needed to complete the lesson are included. (All you need to do is make copies!) Sometimes, a roll of tape or a pair of scissors will be required, but such items are clearly listed at the beginning of each lesson.

The Lessons

Using national educational standards as a guide, the lessons in *Ready to Go Lessons, Grade 4* highlight specific reading and writing strategies. Also included in each lesson are original reading selections, purpose-for-reading questions, a guide to vocabulary development, specific writing assignments, prewriting ideas, organizational guidance for the students, revision and editing instructions, and simple assessment options.

The Assessments

An evaluation sheet is provided at the end of each unit. Every teacher awards points differently, so suggested weights for each objective are not included.

The "possible points" section is left blank. Before making copies, the teacher should fill in how many points the students can earn for mastering each objective. Then, while grading the students' work, teachers can award the points in the "earned points" section.

Extensions

Each lesson comes with an original reading selection. Each reading selection was written with specific lesson objectives in mind, but there are endless variations on what can be done with the reading material.

Lesson One

Objectives

Reading

✔ To identify a biography

✔ To look for compound words

Writing

✔ To write a biography

✔ To organize facts in "time order"

✔ To use interviewing skills to gather information

✔ To get rid of unnecessary information in written work

✔ To follow rules of capitalization

Lesson Summary

The students will read a biography about Chester Greenwood, who invented earmuffs. Then, students will interview a partner in the class in order to write a short biography about that person.

Materials Needed

✴ copies of the reading assignment (page 7)

✴ copies of the writing assignment (page 8)

✴ picture of earmuffs (*optional*)

Part I: The Reading Connection

A. Develop interest in the topic.

Have the students share experiences of when they were very cold. Ask questions such as: "What were you wearing? What do you wish you were wearing? How did you feel?"

B. Encourage students to make predictions about the reading.

Explain to the students that they will be reading a biography about a boy named Chester Greenwood who invented something to help keep people warm in cold weather.

Explain to the students that a biography is a special type of writing: it is written information about someone's life. Tell the students that the title of this biography is "Cold Ears." Have the students predict what might have been invented.

C. Encourage good reading habits.

Remind students that some words look long but are still easy to sound out since they are made up of two little words put together. Explain that these words are called *compound words*. An example of a compound word is *grandmother*. It is made up of the words *grand* and *mother*. Encourage students to look to see if a word is a compound word when trying to sound out a difficult word.

Part I: The Reading Connection *(cont.)*

D. Establish a purpose for reading.

Pass out copies of "Cold Ears" (page 7) for the students to read. Read aloud the questions that the students should answer as they read the story.

E. Define and extend word meaning.

The word *earmuffs* is used in the story, and it might be a new word for some of the students. Tell the students that earmuffs are pieces of material that cover the ears to keep them warm. If possible, show the students a picture of earmuffs.

Explain that *earmuffs* is a compound word. It is made up of two words: *ear* and *muffs*. A muff is a hollow tube made out of material used to keep hands warm. Muffs work by placing the hands inside of the hollow tube.

F. Allow ample time for students to read the selection and reflect upon the assigned questions.

G. Discuss the answers to the reading questions together.

Answers to the questions may vary. However, sample answers are included here:

1. *Why did Chester Greenwood decide to invent earmuffs?* He invented earmuffs because he did not want his ears to get cold while he went skating.
2. *What did Chester use to invent the earmuffs?* He used steel and fur to invent the earmuffs.
3. *Why is "Cold Ears" a biography?* "Cold Ears" is a biography because it gives information about Chester Greenwood's life.

Part II: The Writing Connection

A. Develop interest in the topic.

Ask the students to think about something that they have done that not everyone else in the class has done. Have them think about different foods that they've tried, places that they've gone, and other interesting experiences that they've had. Have students share some of their unique experiences.

B. Explain the writing assignment to the students.

Say, "A biography is factual writings about a person's life. Today, you will be writing a short biography about someone else in the class."

Explain to the students that an interview is a series of questions that you ask someone to find out information. Tell students that they will be interviewing someone in the class and then writing a biography about that person. Place students into pairs for this purpose.

Part II: The Writing Connection *(cont.)*

C. Assist students in gathering information for their biographies.

Distribute the handout on page 8. Read aloud the possible questions that students can ask during their interviews. Have students select at least four questions to ask. Then, have students create at least one question of their own. Allow time for students to complete the interviews.

D. Assist students in organizing the information for their biographies.

Once students have gathered their information, explain that information needs to be written in some sort of order. Explain that one way of organizing information is in the order that things happened (which is called *time order*). Have students examine the facts that they gathered about their partner and try to arrange the facts in a time order. (Note that not all the facts will fall into a time order, but many of the facts will.)

E. Allow writing time.

Give students ample time to organize their facts and write their paragraphs. As they are working, walk around the room and offer guidance.

F. Give students a strategy to help them revise their writing.

Explain to students that details are important when writing, but not every detail needs to be included. Have students look at the list of facts that they gathered to see what facts might not be necessary to include in their biographies. Encourage the students to select at least one fact to exclude from their paragraphs. This will help them practice the habit of weeding out unimportant information.

G. Give students a strategy to help them edit their writing.

Review with the students some rules for capitalization. Have students check to see that they have used these rules correctly in their writing. Students should have capitalized:

✳ the first word in each sentence

✳ a person's first and last name

✳ the name of a city or state

✳ brand names of items.

H. Publish students' ideas.

Have students write their biographies. Read the biographies aloud to the students, without using any names. Have the students guess whose biography is being read.

The Reading Assignment

Directions: Read "Cold Ears." Use complete sentences to answer the questions below.

Cold Ears

Chester Greenwood was born in a small town in Maine in 1858. He was one of six children. He worked hard on his family's farm. Sometimes he made and sold candy to raise extra money.

One day, Chester went ice skating. But, he had to stop skating when his ears got too cold. Since he did not want to stop skating, he tried to find a way to keep his ears warm. He took some steel and fur to his grandmother. He asked his grandmother to sew the fur on the steel. Soon, he was wearing the first pair of earmuffs! He was only 15 years old when he invented earmuffs.

The earmuffs were a big hit. Soon, the town was selling 400,000 earmuffs every year.

Chester went on to invent many more things. Some people say he is one of America's 15 best inventors.

Answer the following questions:

1. Why did Chester Greenwood decide to invent earmuffs? _____

_____

_____

2. What did Chester use to invent the earmuffs? _____

_____

_____

3. Why is "Cold Ears" a biography? _____

_____

_____

The Writing Assignment

Directions: Write a biography about someone else in the class.

> ### Possible Questions to Ask
>
> ✳ Where and when were you born?
>
> ✳ Where have you lived?
>
> ✳ Where have you traveled?
>
> ✳ What do you like to do?
>
> ✳ Can you tell me about your family?
>
> ✳ What are your plans for the future?
>
> ✳ What is something you have done that not everyone else has done?

Other Possible Questions to Ask

1. _____

_____

2. _____

_____

3. _____

_____

The Reading Assignment

Objective	Possible Points	Earned Points
You understand that a biography tells facts about a person's life.		
Total Earned Points:		

The Writing Connection

Objective	Possible Points	Earned Points
You wrote a biography about a person's life.		
You wrote your facts in "time order."		
You left out unnecessary facts in your writing.		
You used rules of capitalization.		
You put effort into the writing process.		
Total Earned Points:		

Additional Teacher Comments: _____

_____

_____

_____

_____

Objectives

Reading

✔ To identify a fairy tale

✔ To read words that end with a silent /e/

Writing

✔ To write using characteristics that could be found in a fairy tale

✔ To use imagery

✔ To identify places to begin new paragraphs

Lesson Summary

The students will read a fairy tale called "The Lonely Prince." Then, the students will write a short story using some characteristics that are commonly found in fairy tales.

Materials Needed

✳ copies of the reading assignment (pages 13–14)

✳ copies of the writing assignment (page 15)

Part I: The Reading Connection

A. Develop interest in the topic.

Have the students list some of their favorite toys that they have had (or wish they had).

B. Encourage students to make predictions about the reading.

1. Tell the students that they will be reading a story called "The Lonely Prince." It is a story about a boy who had all the toys he wanted but still was not happy.

   Explain that this story is an example of a fairy tale. Teach students that many fairy tales have castles, royalty (such as kings), evil characters, magic, make-believe creatures (such as dragons), a problem and solution, a lesson, and sayings like "once upon a time" or "happily ever after."

2. Ask students to make predictions about the story. *Ask:* "Based on the title of the story and what you know about fairy tales, what do you think might happen in this story?" Allow students to give creative answers.

C. Encourage good reading habits.

Remind students that some words end with the letter /e/, but the ending /e/ sound is silent. For example, the /e/ in *creature* is not pronounced. The word *castle* also has a silent /e/. As students read, they should try to remember that all readers must sometimes sound out words. All readers must remember that the /e/ is sometimes silent.

Lesson Two

Part I: The Reading Connection *(cont.)*

D. Establish a purpose for reading.

Pass out copies of "The Lonely Prince" (pages 13–14) for the students to read. Read aloud the instructions to the students.

E. Define and extend word meaning.

The word *dreadful* is used in the story, and it might be a new word for some of the students. Have students help you examine this word for smaller, more familiar words. Students might recognize the word *dread* in the word. When people dread something, they don't want that thing to happen. The word *dreadful* means "awful."

F. Allow ample time for students to read the story and complete the reading assignment.

G. Discuss the answers to the reading assignment together.

Answers to the following questions may vary.

* ✹ *Circle a description of a castle.* Students should have circled the first paragraph of the story.

* ✹ *Put a crown on top of a royal character.* The prince is a royal character.

* ✹ *Draw a scary face next to an evil character.* The dreadful unicorn hunter is an evil character.

* ✹ *Draw a magic wand next to a magical event.* Students might have drawn a wand next to the part of the story where the unicorn disappears or where the unicorn's horn causes the hunter to disappear.

* ✹ *Draw a star around a make-believe creature.* A unicorn is a make-believe creature.

* ✹ *Put a question mark next to a problem that a character has.* The problem is that the prince wants a friend but does not know where to find one.

* ✹ *Put a checkmark next to a lesson that a character learns.* The prince learns that friendship is the most precious gift.

* ✹ *Underline a saying like "once upon a time" or "happily ever after."* The sayings "once upon a time" and "a long, time ago" can be found in the beginning of the story.

* ✹ *Draw a square around a word that ends with a silent /e/.* The words *prince*, *capture*, and *time* are all examples of words that end with a silent /e/.

Part II: The Writing Connection

A. Develop interest in the topic.

List the following on the board: castles, royalty, evil characters, magic, make-believe creatures, a problem and solution, a lesson, and sayings like "once upon a time" or "happily ever after." Then, have students help you list ordinary places on the board (e.g., a classroom, a restaurant, a playground).

B. Explain the writing assignment to the students.

Refer to the lists on the board. Explain to the students that they are going to take an ordinary place and add some fairy tale characteristics to it.

C. Assist students in organizing their fairy tales.

Hand out the writing assignment (page 15) to students. Help the students gather their ideas. Read aloud the instructions and allow students time to answer each question.

D. Allow writing time.

Give students ample time to write their fairy tales. As they are working, walk around the room and offer guidance.

E. Give students a strategy to help them revise their writing.

Explain to the students that descriptive words are important. They allow readers to better picture what the author wishes them to. Descriptive words help writers to share their thoughts and ideas.

One way to add descriptive words in writing is to think about *imagery*. Imagery is words that describe what something . . .

  * looks like   * tastes like   * sounds like
  * feels like   * smells like

For example, instead of just writing, "There was a slide in the park," a writer could write, "The high slide was hot from the sun's rays."

Allow students time to revise their writing using this new skill.

F. Give students a strategy to help them edit their writing.

Remind students that a paragraph is a group of sentences with similar information. For example, one paragraph might have a description of a place, while another paragraph might describe something that happens in the story. Tell students that putting writing into paragraphs helps readers to better understand the writing.

Have students look at their writing in order to find places that might benefit from a new paragraph.

G. Publish students' ideas.

Read parts of the students' fairy tales aloud. Have students raise their hands every time they hear you read an ingredient of a fairy tale.

The Reading Assignment

Directions: Read "The Lonely Prince" below and on page 14. Follow the directions given on page 15.

The Lonely Prince

Once upon a time, a long time ago, there lived a prince in a very big castle. The castle was not so interesting to see from the outside. But there was a lot to see inside this castle.

When people came to visit, the prince demanded that they bring him gifts. So, his castle was filled with toys everywhere. He had golden blocks, fancy puppets, silver bats, and the most wonderful collection of toy magical animals ever seen. He had a toy dragon that breathed fire, stuffed unicorns with diamond-covered horns, and flying beasts that really looked like they flew. People came from near and far to see all of the prince's toys.

One day, a real live unicorn walked through the prince's gates. The prince saw the wonderful creature and said, "I want a unicorn." The unicorn laughed at the prince and replied, "Unicorns are not toys to be owned. We are creatures of the forest and friends only to friends." And with that, the unicorn disappeared.

The prince began to think about what the unicorn had said to him. "I want a friend!" the prince yelled. "Get me a friend!" But the prince's servants did not know where to find a friend for the prince.

Soon, the prince grew angry that he had not been given a friend yet. "I will go find one myself!" he yelled. So the prince went into town and asked several young people to be his friend, but they just bowed down to him and said, "Yes, sir." That was not the prince's idea of a friend.

As he was out searching for a friend, he heard a cry. He turned to see a baby unicorn caught in a trap. The trap had been set by the dreadful unicorn hunter. This hunter tried to capture unicorns in order to steal their horns. The unicorn hunter believed that the horns were the most powerful part of the unicorn.

The Reading Assignment *(cont.)*

The Lonely Prince *(cont.)*

The prince quickly freed the unicorn. Then, he and the unicorn waited. Soon, the hunter arrived, and the prince trapped the hunter in the hunter's own trap. The prince helped the baby unicorn tap the trap with its horn, and the trap and the hunter disappeared.

Then, holding the baby unicorn carefully, he walked through the forest for hours, searching for another unicorn. Soon he found the very unicorn that had walked into his palace.

"Here," said the prince. "Can you take this unicorn to safety?"

"You have proven yourself worthy of our friendship," said the unicorn. "You are a true friend. Thank you."

The next day, the prince's castle was overflowing with unicorns. They had come to meet their new friend. They did not bring toys or presents, only their friendship. And that was the most important gift that the prince had ever been given.

Now re-read the fairy tale and do the following:

✸ Circle the description of the castle.

✸ Put a crown on top of a royal character.

✸ Draw a scary face next to an evil character.

✸ Draw a magic wand next to a magical event.

✸ Draw a star around a make-believe creature.

✸ Put a question mark next to a problem that a character has.

✸ Put a check mark next to a lesson that a character learned.

✸ Underline a saying like "once upon a time" or "happily ever after."

✸ Draw a square around a word that ends with a silent /e/.

The Writing Assignment

Directions: Write a short example of a fairy tale by taking an ordinary place and adding characteristics that can often be found in fairy tales.

Questions to Answer

A. **What ordinary place did you pick to write about in your fairy tale?**

B. **Pick at least four of the following characteristics to add to your story:**

* ✳ royalty
* ✳ evil characters
* ✳ magic
* ✳ make-believe creatures

* ✳ a problem and solution
* ✳ a lesson
* ✳ sayings like "once upon a time" and "happily ever time"

C. **Describe how you will use each ingredient in your story.**

1. _____

_____

2. _____

_____

3. _____

_____

4. _____

_____

Lesson
Two

The Reading Assignment

Teacher Direction: Evaluate the answers to the reading assignment.

Objective	Possible Points	Earned Points
You found characteristics that showed that this story is a fairy tale.		
You drew a square around a word that ended with a silent /e/.		
	Total Earned Points:	

The Writing Connection

Teacher Direction: Evaluate the fairy tales.

Objective	Possible Points	Earned Points
You wrote a story that used at least four characteristics of a fairy tale.		
You used imagery in your writing.		
You used paragraphs to help readers understand your story.		
You put effort into the writing process.		
	Total Earned Points:	

Additional Teacher Comments: _____

_____

_____

_____

_____

Objectives

Reading

✔ To identify a fable

✔ To imagine parts of a story

Writing

✔ To write a mini-fable using a real-life lesson

✔ To use and punctuate dialogue

Lesson Summary

The students will read a fable called "The Best?" Then, students will write a mini-fable using a lesson that they have learned in their lives.

Materials Needed

✱ copies of the reading assignment (pages 20–21)

✱ copies of the writing assignment (page 22)

✱ a picture or example of a walnut (*optional*)

Part I: The Reading Connection

A. Develop interest in the topic.

Ask students to list things that they wished they owned. Then, ask students what they would be willing to trade in order to get those items.

B. Encourage students to make predictions about the reading.

1. Tell the students that they will be reading a story called "The Best?" Explain that this story is an example of a fable. Tell students that fables are stories that teach a lesson. Explain that fables often use animals as the main characters; and the animals in fables often have human characteristics, such as the ability to talk.

2. Ask students to make predictions about the story. *Ask:* "Based on the title of the story and what you know about fables, what do you think this story might be about?" Allow students to give creative answers.

C. Encourage good reading habits.

Remind students that when characters talk, it is called *dialogue*. It is easy to know when characters are speaking because there are *quotation marks* around those words.

Lesson
Three

The Reading Connection *(cont.)*

C. Encourage good reading habits. *(cont.)*

Show students what quotation marks and dialogue look like. For example, show the students the following piece of dialogue from the story:

> *"I'll give you my best walnuts for your house," the squirrel said to the chipmunk family.*

Have the students identify which words are examples of dialogue (i.e., "I'll give you my best walnuts for your house.")

Remind students that as they read, they should give voices to the different characters. Each speaker should sound different. Ask the students to share their thoughts about how this squirrel might sound.

D. Establish a purpose for reading.

Pass out copies of "The Best?" (pages 20–21) for the students to read. Read aloud the questions that the students should answer as they read the story.

E. Define and extend word meaning.

The word *walnut* is used in the story, and it might be a new word for some of the students. If possible, show the students a picture or an example of a walnut. Here is an example of the definition of a walnut: a walnut is a brown nut that grows on trees. It grows with a hard, oval shell around it.

F. Allow ample time for students to read the story and complete the reading assignment.

G. Discuss the answers to the reading assignment together.

1. *Why does the squirrel trade all of his walnuts?* The squirrel trades all of his walnuts because he wants to have the best of everything.

2. *What important lesson does the squirrel learn in the fable?* The squirrel learns that the most important things to have are those things that help you to survive. He learns that having the best is not necessary.

3. *How can you use the lesson that the squirrel learned in your life?* Answers will vary.

4. *Underline an example of dialogue in the story.* There are several different examples of dialogue in the story. Encourage students to look for the quotation marks to help them identify where the dialogue is.

Part II: The Writing Connection

A. Develop interest in the topic.

Ask: "What are some important lessons that you have learned?" As students provide answers, list them on the board.

B. Explain the writing assignment to the students.

For this assignment, students will write a mini-fable about an important lesson they learned.

C. Assist students in organizing their ideas for their mini-fables.

1. Hand out page 22 to students and have them answer the "Get Some Idea" questions on their writing handout.

2. Remind students that in a fable, animals are often the characters in the story. Have students select different animals to use in their stories.

D. Allow writing time.

Give students ample time to write their mini-fables. As they are working, walk around the room and offer guidance.

E. Give students a strategy to help them revise their writing.

Explain to the students that one way to tell a story is to have characters speak. (Remind the students that this is called dialogue.) For example, instead of writing that the squirrel traded his walnuts for the best home, an author can tell the same event using dialogue.

"I'll give you my best walnuts for your house," the squirrel said to the chipmunk family.

"Okay," they answered. The deal was done.

Have the students look at their stories to find places to include dialogue.

F. Give students a strategy to help them edit their writing.

Remind students that quotation marks need to be placed around dialogue to let the reader know what words are being spoken by the characters. Show students what quotation marks look like (" "). Explain that they are placed before the first word being spoken and after the last word being spoken. Here is an example: *"Want to trade?" said the animal.*

(**Note to teacher:** The rules of punctuating dialogue can become more complex. Depending on your students' abilities, you could discuss how to use other punctuation marks within the quotation marks, how punctuation looks different depending on where the speaker is identified, etc. Or, you could keep it simple and just focus on the direct quotes for this exercise.)

G. Publish students' ideas.

Have the students write a clean draft of their mini-fables. Have them draw a picture of an animal in the story to go along with their stories. Read a few of the stories aloud to the class. Display some of the stories in the school building.

The Reading Assignment

Directions: Read "The Best?" below and on page 21. Answer the questions that follow the fable.

The Best?

Once there was a squirrel who liked to have the best of everything. He wanted to have the best house, the best view, the best sounds to listen to, and the best hiding places. But to get the best of everything, he had to find ways to pay for these things.

"I'll give you some of my walnuts for your house, for your house is the best," the squirrel said to the chipmunk family.

"Okay," they answered. The deal was done.

"I'll give you some of my walnuts if you chop down this branch. I need the best view," the squirrel said to the woodpecker.

"Okay," answered the woodpecker. The deal was done.

"I'll give you some of my walnuts if you sing your best songs for me," the squirrel said to the canary.

"Okay," said the canary. The deal was done.

And so life went on this way for the squirrel. He would trade away his walnuts so that he could have the best of everything.

Winter soon came. All the animals settled into their warm, cozy homes, filled with food. It was going to be a good winter. Everyone had plenty of walnuts to eat!

But then, the squirrel realized he had made a mistake. He realized that he had traded what was most important for things that were not so important. He had traded his food, which he needed to live.

Lesson
Three

The Reading Assignment *(cont.)*

The Best? *(cont.)*

So, quickly, before the first snowfall, the squirrel ran around apologizing to all the animals for his poor choices. They were all very forgiving. They were willing to make new trades to the poor little squirrel.

In the end, the squirrel ended up with a warm, cozy little home. It was not the best home, but it had enough walnuts to last the winter. The squirrel could not be happier. Not only did he now have food to survive the winter, but he had learned that having the best was not always the best choice.

Answer the following questions:

1. Why does the squirrel trade all of his walnuts? _____

   _____

   _____

   _____

2. What important lesson does the squirrel learn in the fable? _____

   _____

   _____

   _____

3. How can you use the lesson that the squirrel learned in your life? _____

   _____

   _____

   _____

4. Underline an example of dialogue in the story.

The Writing Assignment

Directions: Write about an important lesson that you have learned.

Get Some Ideas

1. What important lesson have you learned?_____

_____

_____

2. Where were you when you learned the lesson? _____

_____

_____

3. Who helped you to learn this lesson? _____

_____

_____

4. How did you learn this lesson? _____

_____

_____

Select Your Animals

Instead of telling the story as if it happened to you, select animals to be the characters in the story.

The animals in your story are . . .

_____   _____

_____   _____

_____   _____

Lesson
Three

The Reading Assignment

Teacher Direction: Evaluate the answers to the reading assignment.

Objective	Possible Points	Earned Points
You understood the lesson that was taught in the fable.		
You connected the lesson in the fable to your own life.		
You underlined an example of dialogue in the story.		
Total Earned Points:		

The Writing Connection

Teacher Direction: Evaluate the mini-fables.

Objective	Possible Points	Earned Points
You taught a lesson.		
You used animals as your characters.		
You used dialogue to help tell the story.		
You used quotes to punctuate the dialogue.		
You put effort into the writing process.		
Total Earned Points:		

Additional Teacher Comments: _____

_____

_____

_____

Lesson Four

Objectives

Reading

✔ To identify how some myths try to explain the ways of the world
✔ To look for problems and solutions while reading

Writing

✔ To write a myth
✔ To use short, effective descriptions
✔ To identify misspelled words

Lesson Summary

The students will read a myth called "The Great Fall." Then, the students will write a myth about one of the four seasons.

Materials Needed

✱ copies of the reading assignment (pages 28–29)
✱ copies of the writing assignment (page 30)
✱ copies of "Gods and Goddesses from Around the World" (page 31)
✱ dictionaries, spellers, or computers

Part I: The Reading Connection

A. Develop interest in the topic.

Lead a discussion with the students about seasons. Ask the students to discuss their favorite seasons. Have them discuss what they like about each of the different seasons. Have students discuss whether they would prefer to live with one season all of the time or if they would prefer to have different seasons throughout the year.

B. Encourage students to make predictions about the reading.

1. Tell the students that they will be reading a story called "The Great Fall." Explain that this story is an example of a *myth*.

Teach students that some myths are stories that try to answer questions about why things happen in the world the way they do. Myths can be found in different cultures around the world. Many myths that are told today are very old. They were told even before stories were written down. Often, gods and goddesses are main characters in myths. Although some people may still believe in these gods and goddesses, they are most often referred to as "ancient beliefs," or old beliefs.

Part I: The Reading Connection *(cont.)*

B. Encourage students to make predictions about the reading. *(cont.)*

2. Ask students to make predictions about the story. *Ask:* "Based on the title of the story and what you know about myths, what do you think this story might be about?" Allow students to give creative answers.

C. Encourage good reading habits.

Readers should realize that in many stories, a character has a problem of some sort. Once a reader has found the problem in the story, the reader knows to continue to read to look for the solution to the problem. Knowing to look for a problem and knowing to look for a solution helps the reader to know what to look for while reading.

D. Establish a purpose for reading.

Pass out copies of "The Great Fall" (pages 28–29) for the students to read. Read aloud the questions that the students should answer as they read the story.

E. Define and extend word meaning.

The word *sorrow* is used in the story, and it might be a new word for some of the students. Explain that the word *sorrow* means "sadness."

F. Allow ample time for students to read the story and complete the reading assignment.

G. Discuss the answers to the reading assignment together.

1. *What is the little tree's problem in the story?* The little tree's problem is that it is bored of always being green.

2. *How does the wood god try to solve the little tree's problem?* The god of the woods tries to solve the little tree's problem by changing the colors on the tree's leaves.

3. *Is the wood god able to solve the tree's problem?* Answers will vary. The god of the woods is able to change the colors of the leaves, but only for a short time. But the trees seem happy about the change, even if it is not a permanent solution.

4. *What does this myth try to explain?* This myth tries to explain the reason for the fall season.

5. *If you could talk to the little tree, what would you say to it?* Answers will vary.

Part II: The Writing Connection

A. Develop interest in the topic.

Ask questions about the seasons, such as the following:

✸ Why does it snow?

✸ Why does it rain?

✸ Why does it get hotter during the summer than at other times of the year?

Remind students that myths are stories that try to give answers to questions like these—questions that ask about our world and the way things work in our world. Explain that because of our scientific knowledge, we now have the ability to answer many of these questions—but long ago, people did not know the answers to all of these questions. People used to make up stories to explain why things happened the way they did.

Have students ask more of these types of questions. List all of the questions on the board.

B. Explain the writing assignment to the students.

Tell the students that they will be writing myths. They will write a short story that answers a question about the seasons.

Some of the characters in their stories should be gods and goddesses, just like in "ancient" or "olden day" myths. (**Note:** On the student handout on page 31, there is a list of gods and goddesses from different ancient cultures.)

C. Assist students in organizing their myths.

1. Hand out page 30 to the students and help them gather their ideas. Lead students through the steps of identifying their myth's question and answer, selecting their characters, and listing the main events in their story.

   Encourage students to be creative. Remind the students that although we know the answers to some questions about the seasons, people did not always know why or how things happened, so they created stories to explain these things.

2. Remind students that in their stories they should tell where their gods and goddesses are from and what their gods and goddesses do. (See page 31 for a list of gods and goddesses and their countries of origin.)

Part II: The Writing Connection *(cont.)*

D. Allow writing time.

Give students ample time to turn their ideas into a myth. As they are working, walk around the room and offer guidance.

E. Give students a strategy to help them revise their writing.

Tell students that their stories will be short. When writing short stories, there is not always time or space to fully develop characters or places. But, readers still like to know a little bit about the main characters and where the story takes place.

Have students look at their stories and try to find simple ways to give descriptions of their characters. For example, the students could say simply, "The little tree felt sad." This simple sentence gives the reader information about what the tree looks and feels like.

Allow students time to add simple descriptions to their stories.

F. Give students a strategy to help them edit their writing.

Tell students that all writers need help spelling certain words. As writers, they should be aware of what words they know how to spell and what words they are unsure of how to spell.

Have students circle words that they are not sure how to spell. Then, provide students a means—such as computers, spellers, dictionaries, or other writers—of finding the correct spelling of the words.

G. Publish students' ideas.

Make a book with all of the students' myths. Give the book to the media center to display.

The Reading Assignment

Directions: Read "The Great Fall" below. Answer the questions on page 21.

The Great Fall

A sad little tree lived in a forest. The tree had large, green leaves, like all the other trees in the forest. That is why it was so sad.

"Why must my leaves be green, green, green?" asked the little tree. "I am tired of always having green leaves. All year long, my leaves are exactly the same color. When it rains my leaves are green, and when the sun shines my leaves are green. I'm tired of green."

The god of the woods heard the little tree's sorrow. The wood god thought, "If I were always green, I might get a little bored, too." So, he turned the leaves on the little tree bright orange and red.

The little tree was so happy. It waved and danced in the wind. But soon the leaves fell off of the tree, and the tree was bare.

A few months later, the tree began to grow leaves again. The leaves were—as they were before—green, green, green.

The little tree was happy to have leaves back, but after many months of being green, he began to get tired of the green color again.

The god of the woods said, "Every year, if you want, you and all of your cousin trees will turn beautiful colors. But it can only last a short time. Then, your leaves will fall to the ground, and you will be bare for several months. Do not worry, though, for your green leaves will return."

The trees thought about the offer from the wood god. They decided that it would be good to have a change once in awhile. That is why, once a year, many trees experience the changing and falling of the leaves.

The Reading Assignment *(cont.)*

Answer the following questions:

1. What is the little tree's problem in the story? _____

_____

_____

_____

2. How does the wood god try to solve the little tree's problem?_____

_____

_____

_____

3. Is the wood god able to solve the little tree's problem? _____

_____

4. What does this myth try to explain? _____

_____

_____

_____

5. If you could talk to the little tree, what would you say to it? _____

_____

_____

_____

Lesson
Four

The Writing Assignment

Directions: Write a myth. Your myth should answer a question about a season. Your myth should have gods and goddesses as some of the characters, just like "ancient" (or old) myths. Before you begin writing, answer the following questions:

1. What season did you select?

2. What question are you going to answer in your myth?

3. What characters are you going to include in your myth? (You must pick at least one god or goddess.)

Lesson Four

Directions: Use the list below to help you create your myth.

Gods and Goddesses from Around the World

Africa

Abzu—god of water

Adro—god of sky

Arawa—goddess of the moon

Asase Ya—goddess of the Earth

Gwalu—god of rain

Shango—god of thunder

China

Ao—god of the sea

Chang Hs'ien—god of children

Hua-Hsien—goddess of the flower

Meng-T'ien—god of the writing brush

Yao-Wang—god of medicine

Egypt

Hathor—goddess of love and music

Thoth—god of the moon

Bast—goddess of cats

Ma'at—goddess of truth

Greece

Zeus—king of gods

Poseiden—god of the sea

Hades—god of the underworld

Hera—queen of the gods

Demeter—goddess of grains and crops

Hawaii

Kane—god of forest and trees

Kapua—god of trouble-makers

Laka—goddess of clouds and storms

Pele—goddess of volcano fires

Ireland

Bran—god of health

Danu—goddess of water

Flidais—goddess of nature

Angus Og—god of beauty

Japan

Amatsu-Mikaboshi—god of evil

Fujin—god of the wind

Hotei—god of happiness

Kura-Okami—god of rain and snow

Nai-no-Kami—god of earthquakes

Tatsuta-hime—goddess of autumn

Rome

Mars—god of war

Pan—god of the woods

Cupid—goddess of love

Minerva—goddess of wisdom

Vulcan—god of fire

Lesson Four

The Reading Assignment

Teacher Direction: Evaluate the answers to the reading assignment.

Objective	Possible Points	Earned Points
You found the problem and the solution in the myth.		
You found the question that the myth was trying to answer.		
You gave your opinion about the way a character acted in the myth.		
Total Earned Points:		

The Writing Connection

Teacher Direction: Evaluate the myths.

Objective	Possible Points	Earned Points
Your myth answered a question about the seasons.		
You picked at least one god or goddess for your myth. You told who they were and what they did.		
You added simple descriptions to your writing.		
You tried to spell words correctly.		
You put effort into the writing process.		
Total Earned Points:		

Additional Teacher Comments: _____

_____

_____

Lesson Five

Objectives

Reading

✔ To identify important steps of the research process

✔ To make and revise predictions

Writing

✔ To paraphrase writing

✔ To use a direct quote

✔ To cite sources

✔ To brainstorm ideas for possible research topics

✔ To list useable key words for web searching

✔ To identify possible research sources.

Lesson Summary

The students will read a story called "Comical Research," which is about a fourth-grade boy who needs to research a subject for class. Students will fill in the missing words of the story, using words that are important to the research process. Then, students will be asked to help a "student" with some parts of his research project and then to begin thinking about useable ideas for an individual research idea.

Materials Needed

✳ copies of the reading assignment (pages 38–39)

✳ copies of the writing assignment (pags 40–41)

✳ handout (or overhead) entitled "Research Words" (page 37)

Part I: The Reading Connection

A. Develop interest in the topic.

Open up a discussion about comic books. Ask questions, such as the following:

✳ What do know about comic books?

✳ What kind of comic books do you like the best?

✳ If you had the chance to learn more about comic books, what would you want to know?

Part I: The Reading Connection *(cont.)*

B. Encourage students to make predictions about the reading.

Tell students that they will be reading a story called "Comical Research." *Ask:* "Based on the title of the story, what do you predict the story is going to be about?" Answers will vary. Students might respond that the story is about a funny event that happened as someone was researching.

C. Encourage good reading habits.

Remind students that predictions are guesses based on facts. Sometimes, predictions are right, and sometimes they are wrong. Readers must keep changing their predictions as they learn more information or as they realize their predictions are wrong. A wrong prediction is not the sign of a poor reader. But a reader who knows when to change a prediction is more advanced.

D. Establish a purpose for reading.

Tell students that they will be reading a story about a fourth-grader's experience researching comic books. But the story is not complete: there are words missing in the story. The students will need to read the story and try to complete it by selecting the correct words from a list of research words that will be provided to them.

E. Define and extend word meaning.

Students may have had some experience researching in the past, but it is important for students to understand the meaning of the word research to fully understand the goals of the lesson.

1. Write the word *research* on the board. Ask the student if they can find a familiar word within the word *research*. Students should identify the word *search*. Explain that *research* means "to search (or look) for information."

2. Hand out the copies of "Research Words" (page 37) to the students. (If you prefer, you may choose to display this page on an overhead projector.) Read through the list of research words that are provided on the sheet. Try to give examples of each concept, if possible.

F. Allow ample time for students to read the story and complete the reading assignment.

Distribute copies of pages 38–39 to the students. Have them read the story and fill in the blanks with words from the "Research Words" page.

Part I: The Reading Connection *(cont.)*

G. Discuss the answers to the reading assignment together.

Students may have filled in the story as shown here:

Adam was in the fourth grade. His teacher told the class that everyone had to write a research report. Adam could choose to write about any topic. Adam was a little afraid. He had never written a research report. But he knew what his _____*topic*_____ would be: his favorite subject, superhero comic books.

His teacher explained that one way to start the research project was to come up with a list of _____*key words*_____. That way, when Adam went to the library and computer lab, he would know what words to look up to help him find information. Adam began his list: comics, comic books, classic comics, graphic novels, superhero comics, Marvel Comics.

Then, his teacher took the class down to the media center to give the students time to do their _____*research*_____. She said that each student must use at least four different _____*sources*_____. Adam chose to use a computer, an encyclopedia, a book about comic books, and a magazine article.

Adam collected his sources, and began his research. He quickly found a great saying about comic books. In *Batman* #355, entitled "Never Scratch a Cat," Robin said, "We are responsible for each other. That's part of being human—isn't it?" Adam liked this quote. He thought it showed what all of the superheroes believed.

Just then, he heard his teacher say, "Make sure that you do not copy other people's words without giving them credit. That is called _____*plagiarism*_____. If you want to use other people's exact words, then make sure to use a _____*direct quote*_____."

Next, Adam went to a book about classic comics. He found the _____*index*_____ in the back of the book. He used his list of key words to find out where in the book the information he wanted was. Soon, Adam was finding too much information. He could not write everything down. He decided that it was time to _____*summarize*_____ the information that he found. He chose the most important facts and just wrote those down.

Soon, it was Adam's turn on a computer. He found great websites about superhero comic books. He knew he could not write what he found word for word, so he decided to _____*paraphrase*_____ instead.

After a few days in the media center, Adam had all the information he needed. He made a list of all the places he went to find information. His teacher had reminded him that it was important to _____*cite sources*_____.

Finally, he was ready to share what he had learned. He wrote a wonderful _____*research report*_____, but his favorite part was the cover, which he drew to look like a comic book cover.

Part II: The Writing Connection

A. Develop interest in the topic.
Ask: "What are some possible topics for a research report?" List responses on the board.

B. Explain the writing assignment to the students.
If you haven't already, go over the list of research words on page 37 with the students. Then, hand out the writing assignment (pages 40–41). Read aloud the directions with the students. Students may have to complete the last direction on their own paper.

C. Assist students in organizing their paragraphs.
Read the last direction—listed here—aloud to the students again.

✱ *Write a paragraph or more explaining what you already know about your topic and what you would hope to find out as you researched your topic.*

Have the students decide how many directions are really being given. They should respond that they are being asked to do two things in the directions. Have students identify the two questions that they must answer to complete the assignment. They should respond as follows:

✱ *What do you already know about your topic?*

✱ *What do you hope to find out as you research your topic?*

Show students that these questions can help them to organize their writing. Students should group the answers to each individual question together.

D. Allow writing time.
As students write their paragraphs, walk around the room and offer guidance.

E. Give students a strategy to help them revise their writing.
Make sure that students understand how to paraphrase (i.e., rewrite something in their own words). Have students share their paraphrased definitions of graphic novels to show how the definition can be written in different ways. An example of a paraphrased definition of graphic novels is "drawings that tell a serious story."

F. Give students a strategy to help them edit their writing.
Make sure that students know how to use the correct punctuation when citing a source. (**Note:** The method presented in the *MLA Handbook for Writers of Research Papers* is used here, but you may wish to use a different method.)

Author's Last Name, Author's First Name, Middle Initial. <u>Title of Book.</u> *City of Publication: Publisher, Date of Publication.*

Have students identify the different punctuation marks that can be found in the pattern.

Show students an example of a cited source. For example:

Kendle, Endle K. <u>How To Light a Candle.</u> *Waxville: Bright Lights Publisher, 2006.*

G. Publish students' papers.
Have students look at the paragraphs that they wrote and select a part that they feel is especially strong. Have them share that portion of their writing with the class.

Lesson Five

Research Words

cite sources

✳ to list the names of books, magazines, websites, etc., where you find information

direct quote

✳ someone else's exact words

index

✳ a list of topics in the back of some books; includes page numbers to show where in the book the topic is explained.

key words

✳ words to use while researching information

paraphrase

✳ to put someone else's words into your own words

plagiarism

✳ using exact quotes or specific information from a book, magazine, website, etc., without crediting the source

quotation marks (" ")

✳ a set of marks used around dialogue to show that someone wrote or said them

research

✳ to search, or look for, information

source

✳ a place to find information, such as a magazine, encyclopedia, or website

summarize

✳ to shorten someone else's words by writing only the main ideas

topic

✳ subject or idea (what you want to learn more about)

research report

✳ the paragraphs you write after you finish looking for information about your topic so that you can share what you learned

The Reading Assignment

Directions: Read "Comical Research" below and on page 38. Finish the story by filling in the blanks with words from your "Research Words" handout (page 37).

Comical Research

Adam was in the fourth grade. His teacher told the class that everyone had to write a research report. Adam could choose to write about any topic. Adam was a little afraid. He had never written a research report. But he knew what his _____ would be: his favorite subject, superhero comic books.

His teacher explained that one way to start the research project was to come up with a list of _____. That way, when Adam went to the library and computer lab, he would know what words to look up to help him find information. Adam began his list: comics, comic books, classic comics, graphic novels, superhero comics, Marvel comics.

Then, his teacher took the class down to the media center to give the students time to do their _____. She said that each student must use at least four different _____. Adam chose to use a computer, an encyclopedia, a book about comic books, and a magazine article.

The Reading Assignment *(cont.)*

Comical Research *(cont.)*

Adam collected his sources, and began his research. He quickly found a great saying about comic books. In *Batman* #355, entitled "Never Scratch a Cat," Robin said, "We are responsible for each other. That's part of being human—isn't it?" Adam liked this quote. He thought it showed what all of the superheroes believed.

Just then, he heard his teacher say, "Make sure that you do not copy other people's words without giving them credit. That is called _____. If you want to use other people's exact words, then make sure to use a _____."

Next, Adam went to a book about classic comics. He found the _____ in the back of the book. He used his list of key words to find out where in the book the information he wanted was. Soon, Adam was finding too much information. He could not write everything down. He decided that it was time to _____ the information that he found. He chose the most important facts and just wrote those down.

Soon, it was Adam's turn on a computer. He found great websites about superhero comic books. He knew he could not write what he found word for word, so he decided to _____ instead.

After a few days in the media center, Adam had all the information he needed. He made a list of all the places he went to find information. His teacher had reminded him that it was important to _____.

Finally, he was ready to share what he had learned. He wrote a wonderful _____, but his favorite part was the cover, which he drew to look like a comic book cover.

The Writing Assignment (Part I)

Directions: Adam, a fourth-grade boy, needs some help with his research project about comic books. Follow the directions to help Adam.

1. Adam found a definition of "graphic novels" in one of his sources. Adam does not want to plagiarize the definition. The definition reads as follows:

   ✳ *Graphic novels are serious stories that are told through drawings.*

   Show Adam how to use a direct quote: _____

   _____

   _____

   Show Adam how to paraphrase: _____

   _____

   _____

2. Adam used a book called *All About Comics* to do his research. He wrote down the information that he needed so that he could cite his sources. Here is the information that he wrote down:

   ✳ published in 1992

   ✳ written by Ver E. Funny

   ✳ published by Comics, Inc.

   ✳ published in Colorville

   Help Adam cite his source correctly. He must follow this pattern when citing his sources:

   ✳ *Author's last name, Author's first name, Middle Initial.* <u>*Title of Book*</u>*. City of Publication: Publisher, Date of Publication.*

   Now cite Adam's source: _____

   _____

   _____

The Writing Assignment (Part II)

Directions: Imagine that you had to complete a research assignment. Complete the following steps:

1. What topic would you choose? _____

2. What are some key words that you could use?

   _____   _____

   _____   _____

   _____   _____

3. What are three different sources you could use to find information about your topic?

   _____

   _____

   _____

4. Write a paragraph (or more) explaining what you already know about your topic, and what you would hope to find out as you researched your topic.

   _____

   _____

   _____

   _____

   _____

   _____

Lesson Five

The Reading Assignment

Teacher Directions: Evaluate the answers to the reading assignment.

Objective	Possible Points	Earned Points
You understand words related to research.		
Total Earned Points:		

The Writing Connection

Teacher Direction: Evaluate the writing assignment.

Objective	Possible Points	Earned Points
You wrote a direct quote correctly.		
You paraphrased someone else's writing.		
You cited a source using correct punctuation.		
You identified useable key words for a research topic.		
You identified sources for a research topic		
You brainstormed ideas for a research topic.		
You put effort into the writing process.		
Total Earned Points:		

Additional Teacher Comments: _____

_____

_____

_____

Objectives

Reading

✔ To define the word *persuade*

✔ To understand why readers should know when they are reading something persuasive

✔ To understand ways of finding persuasive writing

Writing

✔ To write persuasively

✔ To write a friendly letter using a correct format

Lesson Summary

The students will read a persuasive friendly letter called "No Way." This letter tries to convince students that going on field trips is not a good idea. Then, the students will write a persuasive friendly letter trying to convince the teacher that going on field trips is a good idea.

If you are not really planning a field trip, make sure the students understand that this is a pretend discussion. Explain that you are just using this topic to teach them about persuasion.

Materials Needed

✱ copies of the reading assignment (handout and overhead, pages 47–48)

✱ copies of the writing assignment (page 49)

Part I: The Reading Connection

A. Develop interest in the topic.

Say, "Pretend that we were trying to plan a class field trip. Where would you like to go and why?" Answers will vary, but lead students away from begging ("Please!") and encourage them to come up with reasons that they think different places are good field-trip locations. Ask questions such as the following:

✱ What can we learn from going there?

✱ Why is that a good choice?

✱ How does that fit into what we do at school?

Part I: The Reading Connection *(cont.)*

B. Encourage students to make predictions about the reading.

Tell students that they will be reading a letter that will try to persuade them to understand why you feel that going on a field trip is not a good idea. *Ask:* "What reasons might I use to try to persuade you that going on a field trip is not a good idea?" Students might guess that the letter will say that field trips are hard to plan and expensive.

C. Define and extend word meaning.

The word *persuaded* appears in the reading. Students may never have seen this word. Write the word on the board and help the students learn to decode the word. Explain that *persuaded* means "got others to agree."

D. Encourage good reading habits.

Remind students that one reason that people write is to try to persuade other people to agree with them. Review the definition of the word *persuade.* Then ask the following questions:

✸ *Who writes things down to try to persuade you to do things?* Answers might include advertisers on television, magazine advertisements, people trying to sell specific products, etc.

✸ *Why is it important for you to understand when you are reading something persuasive?* Persuasive writing might be wrong, be an opinion (not fact), or show only facts that will help make one side of the argument stronger.

✸ *What could the problem be if someone reads something persuasive but does not realize it is persuasive?* The problem with reading something persuasive and not knowing it is persuasive is that the reader could think that the information they are reading is factual. Also, persuasive writing does not always discuss all sides of an issue. Persuasive writing might get you to do or buy something that you don't want to do or buy.

✸ *How can you tell when you are reading something persuasive?* Persuasive writers will try to get you to agree with them by giving you reasons why their arguments are right.

E. Establish a purpose for reading.

Distribute copies of the letter on page 47 and the questions on page 48 for the students to read. Read aloud the questions that the students should answer as they read the story.

F. Allow ample time for students to read the story and complete the reading assignment.

Part I: The Reading Connection *(cont.)*

G. Discuss the answers to the reading assignment together.

1. *What are some reasons that the letter gives for not wanting to go on field trips?* Some reasons that the letter gives are that field trips are hard to plan, field trips cost money, and that it is hard to choose a place that will make everyone happy.

2. *What is the purpose of the letter?* The purpose of the letter is to persuade the class that field trips are not a good idea.

3. *What does your teacher think schools should do instead of going on field trips?* My teacher thinks that showing videos of interesting or famous places is a good substitute for going on field trips.

4. *Do you agree with your teacher's letter? Why or why not?* Answers will vary.

Part II: The Writing Connection

A. Develop interest in the topic.

Read the letter on page 47 aloud to the students. Then, if you have not completed **"Part I: D. Encourage Good Reading Habits,"** do so before continuing the lesson.

B. Explain the writing assignment to the students.

Tell students that they are going to be writing a friendly letter to their teacher trying to persuade him or her that going on field trips is a good idea.

C. Assist students in organizing their persuasive letters.

Hand out copies of page 49. Help the students gather their ideas. *Ask:* "What are some reasons that you think field trips are a good idea?" Write student responses on the board. Students can select from this list or create their own reasons. Have them write their selected reasons on their handout. (**Note:** There is a chart on the student handout. The chart will be addressed during the revision process.)

D. Allow writing time.

Give students ample time to begin writing their letters. As they are working, walk around the room and offer guidance.

Lesson Six

Part II: The Writing Connection *(cont.)*

E. Give students a strategy to help them revise their writing.

Explain to the students that sometimes when writers revise, they look for places to add information. When doing persuasive writing, writers should look to see where they can make their argument stronger.

One way to make a persuasive argument stronger is to figure out what people might say in an argument against your point. For example, what reasons did the letter give for not wanting to go on a field trip? Write those reasons on the chart. (See the Writing Assignment on page 49).

* ✴ *Field trips are hard to plan.*

* ✴ *Field trips can be expensive.*

* ✴ *It is hard to decide where to go on a field trip.*

Then, try to come up with ways to try to make those reasons seem less of a problem. For example, field trips are hard to plan, but there are many students who are willing to help plan the trip.

Have students complete their charts. Then, allow students time to revise their letters, using this new persuasive skill. Give students time to address at least one of the teacher's concerns in their letters.

F. Give students a strategy to help them edit their writing.

Place the letter from page 47 on the overhead. Identify the different parts of the friendly letter. Have students format their letters to look the same as this one.

* ✴ The heading is indented and includes the sender's return address.

* ✴ Skip a line after the return address and center the date.

* ✴ Add the greeting and follow it with a comma (for example, "Dear Sally,").

* ✴ Skip a line and indent to begin each paragraph.

* ✴ Indent the closing and follow it with a comma (for example, "Sincerely," "Yours truly," "Thank you," etc.).

* ✴ Handwrite a signature.

* ✴ Print the name of the sender.

Give students time to edit, using the new skill.

G. Publish students' ideas.

Have students select their strongest persuasive paragraph from their letter. Have students read that paragraph aloud to the class.

The Reading Assignment

Directions: Read the letter below and answer the questions on page 48.

1 School Lane

Eduville, Indiana 00000

April 23, 2007

Dear Class,

Some people think that field trips are an important part of learning. Many students have been asking me when we can go on a field trip. But I wanted to let you know that I think that school field trips are a terrible idea.

One reason that field trips are such a terrible idea is that they take so much planning. A place for the trip needs to be picked. Letters need to be sent home. Dates need to be arranged. Buses need to be ordered. Lunches need to stored or bought. The nurse needs to be contacted. Doing all that takes a lot of time.

Another reason that field trips are a terrible idea is that they can cost a lot of money. Admission cost money. Buses cost money. And students often want to spend extra money while they are on the trip.

The last reason why field trips are such a terrible idea is that there are so many places to possibly go. It is too hard to decide on one place to visit. No matter where we go, some people will not like the choice.

I think it would be better if schools stopped going on field trips. We could show videos of interesting and famous places instead.

I hope that I have persuaded you that field trips are not a good idea. What do you think?

Sincerely,

Your Teacher

Your Teacher

P.S. Please write back.

The Reading Assignment *(cont.)*

Answer the following questions:

1. What are some reasons that the letter gives for not wanting to go on field trips?

2. What is the purpose of the letter?

3. What does your teacher think schools should do instead of going on field trips?

4. Do you agree with your teacher's letter? Why or why not?

Lesson Six

The Writing Assignment

Directions: Write a persuasive letter to your teacher about why school field trips are a good idea.

Think and Write

What are reasons that taking a school field trip is a good idea?

_____

_____

_____

_____

Why does your teacher think that taking a field trip is *not* a good idea?	What can you say to help your teacher feel better about each concern?

The Reading Assignment

Teacher Direction: Evaluate the answers to the reading question.

Objective	Possible Points	Earned Points
You found persuasive reasons listed in the letter.		
Total Earned Points:		

The Writing Connection

Teacher Direction: Evaluate the friendly letters.

Objective	Possible Points	Earned Points
You gave reasons to make your argument strong.		
You discussed at least one concern that your teacher presented.		
You put effort into setting up a friendly letter correctly.		
You put effort into the writing process.		
Total Earned Points:		

Additional Teacher Comments: _____

_____

_____

_____

_____

_____

Objectives

Reading

✔ To personally connect with characters, events, and feelings while reading a story

Writing

✔ To connect personal experiences, events, and feelings to those in a story

✔ To tell a story with a beginning, middle, and end

✔ To use paragraphs purposefully and correctly

Lesson Summary

The students will read a story called "The Green Lady," which is about a boy who becomes disappointed when he misses the last boat to see the Statue of Liberty. Students will be guided to make personal connections to the story. Then, students will write a narrative about a time that they felt disappointed.

Materials Needed

✱ copies of the reading assignment (pages 55–56)

✱ copies of the writing assignment (page 57)

✱ copies of "Common Storytelling Words" (page 58)

Part I: The Reading Connection

A. Develop interest in the topic.

Ask students to discuss different places that they've been on vacation.

B. Encourage students to make predictions about the reading.

1. Tell the students that they will be reading a story called "The Green Lady."

2. Ask students to make predictions about the story. *Ask:* "Based on the title of the story, what do you think this story could be about?" Allow students to give creative answers.

Part I: The Reading Connection *(cont.)*

C. Encourage good reading habits.

Tell students that when reading a story, readers can try to connect their own lives and experiences to those in the story. They can try to connect to . . .

* ✱ a *character* by thinking of similar people they know

* ✱ an *event* by thinking of similar things they have experienced

* ✱ a *place* by thinking of similar places they have been to or seen pictures of

* ✱ a *feeling* by thinking of similar feelings that they have had.

For example, if they are reading a story that takes place in a classroom, they could picture a classroom that they have seen. If they are reading about a character who is excited, they can remember a time when they were excited.

By connecting their own lives to a story they are reading, they can do the following:

* ✱ *better picture the story in their minds*

* ✱ *begin to understand why the characters do what they do, feel the way they feel, or act the way they act.*

For example, students might be able to understand why a sad character started to cry in a story if they remember a time when they were sad and started to cry.

D. Establish a purpose for reading.

Pass out copies of "The Green Lady" (pages 55–56) for the students to read. Read aloud the questions that the students should answer as they read the story.

E. Define and extend word meaning.

The phrase *double-decker bus* is used in the story, and it might be a new concept for some of the students. Before asking students to complete the reading assignment, write the phrase on the board. Help the students read the words. Then, help the students understand the meaning of the phrase.

A double-decker bus is a bus with two layers of seats. There are stairs in the bus that allow people to climb up to the second floor.

F. Allow ample time for students to read the story and complete the reading assignment on pages 55 and 56.

Part I: The Reading Connection *(cont.)*

G. Discuss the answers to the reading assignment together.

1. *Why does Joshua feel excited in the story?* Joshua feels excited because he is in New York City and he is going to see the Statue of Liberty.

2. *Why does Joshua feel disappointed in the story?* Joshua feels disappointed when he finds out that he missed the last ferry that went to see the Statue of Liberty.

3. *What is one other emotion that Joshua feels in the story?* Answers will vary, but might include sad, amazed, or thrilled.

4. *When have you felt an emotion that Joshua felt in the story?* Answers will vary.

Part II: The Writing Connection

A. Develop interest in the topic.

1. Have students share experiences when they have felt disappointed. Encourage thinking by asking question such as the following:

   ✳ Did you ever think that something was going to happen and then feel disappointed when it didn't?

   ✳ Did you ever think something was going to happen a certain way, and then felt disappointed when it didn't?

   ✳ Did you ever want something and then feel disappointed when you could not have it?

   ✳ Did you ever feel disappointed in the way someone else acted?

   ✳ Did you ever feel disappointed in yourself?

2. Then, if students have not already read "The Green Lady," read the story aloud. As you are reading, have students listen to find out why Joshua felt disappointed.

B. Explain the writing assignment to the students.

Explain to the students that they will be writing a story about a time when they felt disappointed.

Part II: The Writing Connection *(cont.)*

C. Assist students in organizing their stories.

Distribute copies of the writing assignment on page 57 to students. Help the students organize their ideas. Read aloud the questions on their writing-assignment handout and allow students time to answer each question. As students begin to gather their ideas, have them share them with the class.

D. Allow writing time.

Give students ample time to write their paragraphs. As they are working, walk around the room and offer guidance.

E. Give students a strategy to help them revise their writing.

Remind students that their stories should have a beginning, a middle, and an end. Explain that there are some words that can help the story flow from the beginning to the middle to the end.

Hand out "Common Storytelling Words" (page 58). Have students use at least three of these words, or similar words, in their stories.

F. Give students a strategy to help them edit their writing.

Show students the story "The Green Lady." Have students count the different paragraphs that were written. Explain that writers use different paragraphs to help a reader understand the story. Sometimes, new paragraphs tell the reader that something new is happening in the story.

You can start a new paragraph to show a change in . . .

* action/event   * place

* character   * mood

* time   * description

Show students how to indent a paragraph. Give students time to edit their papers using this skill.

G. Publish students' ideas.

Have students examine their papers to select their best paragraph. Perhaps the paragraph is interesting, has good descriptions, has a good lesson, etc. Have students read the selected paragraph aloud to the class.

The Reading Assignment

Directions: Read "The Green Lady" below and on page 56. Answer the questions that follow.

The Green Lady

Joshua was thrilled. He was finally going to New York City. He had seen pictures of it. He had studied all about it in school. He had even seen parts of New York City in movies. But he had never seen it for himself.

He was looking forward to seeing the tall buildings that reached for the sky. He wanted to see Times Square. But most of all, he wanted to see The Statue of Liberty. The Statue of Liberty, he knew, was a symbol of freedom in the United States. He could not wait to take the boat ride to see her up close.

But first his family took a tour on the top of an open-topped, double-decker bus. It was a breathtaking way to see the city. Although he had a cool view from "up high," New York City was still much higher up than he was! It was amazing how tall those buildings were! "Be careful!" his mom called out. Luckily, he ducked just in time: there was one streetlight that was very low and close to his head.

After the tour, Joshua walked with his family through a part of the city. Then, he found a T-shirt that said, "I love NY." It was just his size, and he bought it.

Now it was time to head for the ferry to see the great statue. As they turned a corner, he caught his first glimpse of her. It was an amazing and exciting experience—just like he knew it would be.

The Reading Assignment *(cont.)*

The Green Lady *(cont.)*

Just then, Joshua saw a sign saying that the last ferry had left for the day. His heart sank. He was so close, but he was not going to be able to get any closer. His eyes started to fill with tears.

"I'm sorry," said his mother. "I did not know that the last ferry left this early. We'll have to try again next time." She reached down and gave Joshua a hug.

Joshua was disappointed, but he knew he would come back . . . someday.

Answer the following questions:

1. Why does Joshua feel excited in the story?_____

_____

_____

2. Why does Joshua feel disappointed in the story? _____

_____

_____

3. What is one other emotion that Joshua feels in the story? _____

_____

_____

4. When have you felt an emotion that Joshua felt in the story? _____

_____

_____

The Writing Assignment

Directions: Write a story about a time that you felt disappointed. Before writing, answer these questions:

1. When have you felt disappointed?

2. Where does your story take place? Who are the characters in your story?

3. How does your story start?

4. What happens in the middle of your story?

5. How does your story end?

Common Storytelling Words

Beginning Storytelling Words

* Once there was . . .

* It all began when . . .

* One day . . .

* One morning . . .

* There was a time when . . .

* One time . . .

Middle-of-the-Story Words

* Then . . .

* After that . . .

* Soon . . .

* Next . . .

* There was also . . .

* Also . . .

* The next day . . .

* Several days later . . .

* As the day continued . . .

Ending Storytelling Words

* In the end . . .

* So . . .

* At the end of the day . . .

* When it was all over . . .

* When it was time to leave . . .

* Finally . . .

* Later . . .

* Since . . .

* After that . . .

* Afterward . . .

* By that time . . .

* Next time . . .

The Reading Assignment

Teacher Direction: Evaluate the answers to the reading questions.

Objective	Possible Points	Earned Points
You connected to the feelings of a character in a story.		
	Total Earned Points:	

The Writing Connection

Teacher Direction: Evaluate the stories.

Objective	Possible Points	Earned Points
You wrote a story about a time when you were disappointed.		
You used special storytelling words to help tell your story.		
Your story had different paragraphs.		
Your story had a beginning, middle, and ending.		
You put effort into the writing process.		
	Total Earned Points:	

Additional Teacher Comments: _____

_____

_____

_____

_____

Organizational Patterns   Lesson Eight   *Teacher Instructions*

Objectives

Reading

✔ To identify common patterns authors use to tell information (compare/contrast, cause/effect, time order, idea/support, problem/solution)

Writing

✔ To write a persuasive, friendly letter using common patterns of telling information (compare/contrast, cause/effect, time order, idea/support, problem/solution)

✔ To write a friendly letter in the correct format

✔ To choose words to write for a specific person (audience)

Lesson Summary

The students will read a story called "Oh, Brother!" and identify common organizational patterns that the author uses to tell information. Students will then use the common organizational patterns of telling information to write a persuasive letter that details their ideas for a relaxing time.

(**Note:** Lesson Twelve (pages 99–107) continues to focus on these same patterns of compare/contrast, cause/effect, time order, idea/support, problem/solution. Specifically, Lesson Twelve focuses on how these patterns are used in textbooks to tell information.)

Materials Needed

✱ copies of the reading assignment (pages 64–66)

✱ copies of the writing assignment (pages 68–69)

✱ handout or overhead of "Common Patterns Used to Tell Information" (page 67)

✱ handout or overhead of "Friendly-Letter Format" (page 70)

Part I: The Reading Connection

A. Develop interest in the topic.

Ask students if they have ever felt surprised. Give students an opportunity to share their experiences.

B. Encourage students to make predictions about the reading.

1. Tell the students that they will be reading a story called "Oh, Brother!"

2. Ask students to make predictions about the story. *Ask:* "Based on the title of the story, what do you think this story might be about?" Allow students to give creative answers.

Lesson Eight

Part I: The Reading Connection *(cont.)*

C. Encourage good reading habits.

Distribute copies (or display overhead) of page 67. Explain that many times, authors give information in patterns. Some common patterns are as follows:

* **Compare and Contrast**—Writers tell how things are the same and how they are different.

   Example: Both recipes were easy to follow. One recipe needed an oven, and the other recipe needed the stove.

* **Time Order**—Writers tell things in the order that they happened or will happen.

   Example: First I need to buy new shoes, and then I'll see if I can find a new shirt.

* **Cause and Effect**—Writers tell how or why something happened or will happen.

   Example: If you spend all of your money now, you won't have any left to buy ice cream later.

* **Idea and Support**—Writers tell an idea and then explain it.

   Example: I think I am going to ask my dad to help me build my model rocket because it looks very hard to put together.

* **Problem and Solution**—Writers tell a problem and then tell how to solve it.

   Example: I am tired, so I am going to take a nap.

   Explain that these patterns can be found in all sorts of writing. They can be found in stories, textbooks, newspapers, etc.

D. Establish a purpose for reading.

Pass out copies of "Oh, Brother!" (pages 64–65) for the students to read. Read aloud the questions (page 66) that the students should answer as they read the story.

E. Define and extend word meaning.

The word *assistance* is used in the story, and it might be a new word for some of the students. Before asking student to complete the reading assignment, write the word on the board. Help the students read the word. Show the students that the word *assist* is in the word. Explain that *assistance* means "aid" or "help."

assistance

F. Allow ample time for students to read the story and complete the reading assignment on page 66.

Part I: The Reading Connection *(cont.)*

G. Discuss the answers to the reading assignment together.

Answers will vary; the following are suggested answers:

1. *Why does James want to throw a party for Jarred?* James wants to throw a party for his brother because it is his birthday, parties are fun to plan, he wants to do something special for his brother, and he feels that Jarred deserves to have a party.

2. *Why is James surprised at the end of the story?* James is surprised at the end of the story because Jarred has planned a party for James, too.

3. Students should have followed these directions to locate patterns in the text:

   ✳ *Place a funny face next to the paragraph that compares and contrasts ideas.*
   Paragraph five compares and contrasts ideas.

   ✳ *Circle the paragraph that tells ideas in a time order.*
   Paragraph four tells ideas in a time order.

   ✳ *Put a checkmark next to the paragraph that shows cause and effect.*
   Paragraph six shows cause and effect.

   ✳ *Draw a star next to the paragraph that tells an idea and supports it.*
   Paragraph two shows idea and support.

   ✳ *Put a question mark next to the paragraph that tells problems and solutions.*
   Paragraph three shows problems and solutions.

Part II: The Writing Connection

A. Develop interest in the topic.

Have students think about a time that they were surprised by someone; have them think of a time when they surprised someone else.

B. Explain the writing assignment to the students.

Tell the students that they will be writing a letter to someone telling about the time that they were surprised or surprised someone.

C. Assist students in organizing their writing assignment.

1. Hand out the writing assignment on pages 68–69. Remind students that newspapers, textbooks, magazines, and stories all have common ways of presenting information (e.g., compare and contrast, time order, cause and effect, idea and support, problem and solution). Just as good readers learn to look for these patterns as they read, good writers learn to use these patterns to clearly tell information.

2. Lead the students through the questions on their writing-assignment handouts. Help students tackle the different writing patterns presented.

Part II: The Writing Connection *(cont.)*

D. Allow writing time.

Give students ample time to write their letters. Remind students to use at least four of the patterns of telling information in their letters.

E. Give students a strategy to help them revise their writing.

Remind students that when people speak, they change the way they speak depending on who they are talking to at the time. For example, when people talk to their bosses at work, they do not speak the same way they do when they are talking to their siblings.

Have students discuss who they use more formal language with (e.g., teachers, friends' parents, coaches, principal) and who they speak to in a more relaxed way (e.g., friends, siblings, cousins).

Tell students that when they write, their word choice should also change depending on who they are writing to, or the *audience* of the writing. Have students think about who they are writing their letters to and how their wording should change as a result.

F. Give students a strategy to help them edit their writing.

Distribute copies of (or display an overhead of) page 70. Identify the different parts of the friendly letter.

* The heading is indented and includes the sender's return address.

* Skip a line after the return address and center the date.

* Add the greeting and follow it with a comma (for example, "Dear Sally,").

* Skip a line and indent to begin each paragraph.

* Indent the closing and follow it with a comma (for example, "Sincerely," "Yours truly," "Thank you," etc.).

* Handwrite a signature.

* Print the name of the sender.

Give students time to edit, using the new skill.

G. Publish students' ideas.

Have students select their favorite paragraphs from their letters. The selected paragraph should use one of the patterns of telling information that was discussed in class. Have students practice reading that paragraph aloud to a partner, then to a small group. Remind students to focus on reading slowly and loudly. Then, have each student read the selected paragraph aloud to the class. Have the class identify the pattern that was used.

The Reading Assignment

Directions: Read "Oh Brother!" below and on page 65. Answer the questions and follow the directions on page 66.

Oh, Brother!

James and Jarred were brothers. Like most brothers, they sometimes played together and they sometimes fought with each other. But all in all, they really cared about each other.

Jarred was having a birthday. James decided that he wanted to do something special for Jarred. Suddenly, he had an idea. After thinking about the idea for some time, he ran to find his parents. He asked them if he could throw a party for his brother. "A birthday party would be great," he explained. "It would be fun to plan, many people would like to celebrate with Jarred, and Jarred deserves this party.

"I know that there is a lot of work that needs to go into planning a party. Jarred's birthday is soon. It will be hard to get everything done in time. But I've already thought about that problem. I have friends who would be willing to help. I've got everything all planned out already.

"First," he continued, "I will make the invitations on the computer. We can mail them out tomorrow. Then, this weekend, my friend will help me cut the grass. After that, we can all clean the house together. Then, on the day before the party, we can go food shopping. On the day of the party, we will do all the last-minute things. If we keep it simple, we can get it done."

"Are you sure you want to do this?" James's mother asked, "We could just take him to the movies instead. You know how he loves movies!" But James quickly replied, "Both a movie and a party are fun ideas. But we often go to the movies. A party is different. It is special."

"You know," his mom replied, "if we have a party, there is a lot of work that has to be done after the party, as well. The house will have to be cleaned up from the party, and thank-you notes will have to be written to everyone who offered you assistance. Plus, things can get ruined. Parties create messes!"

The Reading Assignment *(cont.)*

Oh, Brother! *(cont.)*

All of a sudden, James heard a funny noise in the other room. It sounded like giggling. James went to see what the noise was.

"Surprise!" his friends yelled.

"What is going on here?" asked James, confused.

"I think you are a great brother," explained Jarred, "so I wanted to surprise you with a party. "

"But, it is not my birthday," said James.

"I know," said Jarred. "That is why it is such a good surprise."

"Oh, brother!" sighed James happily.

The Reading Assignment *(cont.)*

Answer the following questions:

1. Why does James want to throw a party for Jarred? _____

_____

_____

_____

_____

2. Why is James surprised at the end of the story? _____

_____

_____

_____

_____

3. Search for patterns the author uses to tell information and follow these directions:

   ✸ Place a funny face (☺) next to the paragraph that *compares and contrasts* ideas.

   ✸ Circle the paragraph that tells ideas in a *time order*.

   ✸ Put a checkmark (✔) next to the paragraph that shows *cause and effect*.

   ✸ Draw a star (★) next to the paragraph that tells an *idea and supports it*.

   ✸ Put a question mark (?) next to the paragraph that tells *problems and solutions*.

Common Patterns Used to Tell Information

Compare and Contrast

✳ Writers tell how things are the same and how things are different.

Here is an example: Both recipes were easy to follow. One recipe needed an oven, and the other recipe needed the stove.

Time Order

✳ Writers tell things in the order that they happened or will happen.

Here is an example: First I need to buy new shoes, and then I'll see if I can find a new shirt.

Cause and Effect

✳ Writers tell how or why something happened or will happen.

Here is an example: If you spend all your money now, you won't have any left to buy ice cream later.

Idea and Support

✳ Writers tell an idea, and then explain the idea.

Here is an example: I think I am going to ask my dad to help me build my model rocket because it looks very hard to put together.

Problem and Solution

✳ Writers tell a problem and then tell how to solve the problem.

Here is an example: I am tired, so I am going to take a nap.

The Writing Assignment

Directions: Write a letter to someone telling them about one of the following:

✳ a time that you were surprised

✳ a time that you surprised someone else.

Before you write, organize your ideas using writing patterns. (Select any *four* of the five listed below and on page 69.)

○ **Time Order**—*Writers tell things in the order that they happened or will happen.*

For example, tell the events leading up to the surprise and how the surprise happened.

_____

_____

_____

_____

_____

○ **Idea and Support**—*Writers tell an idea and then explain it.*

For example, why was there a surprise?

_____

_____

_____

_____

_____

The Writing Assignment *(cont.)*

○ **Cause and Effect**—*Writers tell how or why something happened or will happen.*

For example, what made the surprise happen?

_____

_____

_____

_____

_____

○ **Problem and Solution**—*Writers tell a problem and then tell how to solve it.*

For example, what problems had to be solved?

_____

_____

_____

_____

_____

○ **Compare and Contrast**—*Writers tell how things are the same and how things are different.*

For example, how was this similar or different to other surprises?

_____

_____

_____

_____

_____

Friendly-Letter Format

Street Number and Address

City, State and Zip Code

Today's Date

Dear _____,

Skip a line and indent the first paragraph.

Skip a line and indent the next paragraph.

Continue to skip lines and indent each paragraph until you are finished writing your letter.

Sincerely,

Your Signature

Your Printed Name

Teacher Direction: Evaluate the answers to the reading assignment.

Objective	Possible Points	Earned Points
You understood the basic story.		
You found different patterns that the author used to tell information in a story.		
Total Earned Points:		

The Writing Connection

Teacher Direction: Evaluate the friendly letter.

Objective	Possible Points	Earned Points
You wrote about a surprise.		
You told information in at least four different ways.		
You thought about the person you were writing to, and you chose words for that person.		
You set up your letter correctly.		
You put effort into the writing process.		
Total Earned Points:		

Additional Teacher Comments: _____

_____

_____

_____

_____

Lesson Nine

Objectives

Reading

✔ To identify personification, alliteration, onomatopoeia, simile, metaphor, imagery, and hyperbole

Writing

✔ To write creatively using personification, alliteration, onomatopoeia, simile, metaphor, imagery, and hyperbole

✔ To select a writing format

✔ To identify when and how to break grammar rules

Lesson Summary

The students will study personification, alliteration, onomatopoeia, simile, metaphor, imagery, and hyperbole. The students will identify examples of each in a poem called "My Buddy, My Bike." Then, the students will complete a creative-writing assignment about an object, using their own examples of personification, alliteration, onomatopoeia, simile, metaphor, imagery, and hyperbole. Students will also be introduced to some of the other fun elements of creative writing, such as breaking the rules of grammar and writing in creative formations.

Materials Needed

✱ copies of the reading assignment (page 78)

✱ copies of the writing assignment (page 79)

✱ copies of "Common Tricks to Write Creatively" (page 77)

Part I: The Reading Connection

A. Develop interest in the topic.

Tell students that they are going to read a poem about bikes, called "My Buddy, My Bike." Individually or in small groups, have the students create a list of possible words that might be in a poem about bikes. Answers will vary but might include *gears, wheels, handles, brakes,* and *helmet.*

B. Encourage students to make predictions about the reading.

1. Explain to the students that they have already made predictions about words that they might find in the poem.

Part I: The Reading Connection *(cont.)*

2. Ask students to make more predictions about the poem, sharing what they know about poetry. *Say:* "Think about what you know about poems and poetry. What might this poem look like and sound like as you read it?" Allow students to share their knowledge of poetry. Answers might include rhyming words, short sentences, rhythms, etc.

   Point out that poetry is a way of using words as art. Explain that poetry does not have rules that must be followed, which is one reason why people find poetry so creative and interesting. For example, poetry does not have to have rhyming words, punctuation, capital letters, or even be written in straight lines. It is a free form of writing.

C. Encourage good reading habits.

Explain that there are some common tricks that authors use when they write creatively. Understanding these common creative tricks makes reading more fun and easier to understand.

Hand out copies of "Common Tricks to Write Creatively" (page 77) to students. On the blank lines provided, have students write examples of writing tricks as you discuss them in class. Answers may vary, but examples are as follows:

Personification (*making something that is not alive act like a human*)

❋ *Example:* The writing screamed at me.

Alliteration (*using the same consonant sounds several times*)

❋ *Example:* Meeting in the meadow were many mini mice.

Onomatopoeia (*words that are meant to imitate sounds*)

❋ *Example:* Plop!

Metaphor (*a comparison*)

❋ *Example:* The message was heavier than a load of bricks.

Simile (*a type of metaphor that uses the words "like" or "as"*)

❋ *Example:* He was as quiet as a feather falling.

Imagery (*words that tell what something looks like, smells like, feels like, sounds like, or tastes like*)

❋ *Example:* The sunset looked like a rainbow of fall colors.

Hyperbole (*a large exaggeration*)

❋ *Example:* I am so tired I could sleep for a week.

Part I: The Reading Connection *(cont.)*

D. Establish a purpose for reading.

Pass out copies of "My Buddy, My Bike" for the students to read. Have students find an example each of personification, alliteration, onomatopoeia, simile, metaphor, imagery, and hyperbole within the poem.

E. Define and extend word meaning.

The word *turbulence* is used in the story, and it might be a new word for some of the students. Write the word on the board and help students to read the word. Point out that /ence/ is a common letter combination found at the end of words.

Tell the students to imagine that they are sitting on a plane. Have them all lean slightly to the right, then slightly to the left, as they imagine that the plane is leaning. Then, have them bump a little in their seats. Explain that the bumping is called turbulence.

F. Allow ample time for students to read the poem and complete the reading assignment.

Hand out page 78. Depending on the classroom situation, you might want to have the students complete this assignment in small groups.

G. Discuss the answers to the reading assignment together.

Answers to these reading-assignment questions may vary. The following are examples:

Personification: "My bike, a soldier, brave and true."

Alliteration: "My Buddy, My Bike" and "Peddling down a perfect path, pushing with power, then pausing with pride."

Onomatopoeia: "Huffing and puffing to get more air, breaks squeaking, gears clicking, tires bumping, gears grinding."

Simile: "...while moving as fast as a cross-country train" and "Feeling like turbulence in a plane."

Metaphor: "My bike, a soldier, brave and true. My helmet, my armor, protecting me, too."

Imagery: "Weaving my way through a big city, stopping and going, slowing and speeding" and "Gliding through forests on muddy trails."

Hyperbole: "'Forever!' I cried."

Part II: The Writing Connection

A. Develop interest in the topic.

Create a list of objects on the board with the students help. You may choose to use the following as examples:

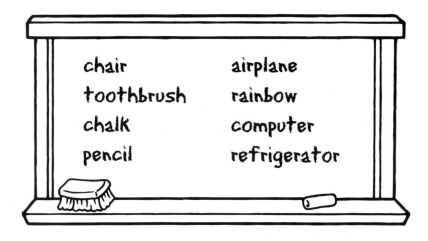

chair	airplane
toothbrush	rainbow
chalk	computer
pencil	refrigerator

Then, have each student select one of the objects on the board (or an object that is not listed).

Depending on the classroom situation, you might choose instead to complete the writing assignment as a class (using one object) or in small groups (using selected or assigned objects).

B. Explain the writing assignment to the students.

Explain to the students that they are going to do some creative writing about their objects, using some common creative writing tricks that authors use. (Since the reading selection on page 78 is a poem, you may wish to explain to students that they are not expected to write a poem.)

If you did not complete the reading portion of this lesson, you will need to review the "Common Tricks to Write Creatively" handout. (See **Part I: The Reading Connection, Step C,** for further instructions.)

C. Assist students in organizing their creative writing assignment.

Hand out the writing assignment on page 79. Help the students gather their ideas. Guide the students through the writing-assignment handout.

D. Allow writing time.

Have students begin to put their creative-writing ideas together. Move on to the next step rather quickly, though. (The next step, **Step E,** will give the students an idea of the different formats they can use when writing creatively.)

Part II: The Writing Connection *(cont.)*

E. Give students a strategy to help them revise their writing.

Explain to the students that what they write is important, but how they choose to present the information is important, as well. Tell the students that people write in many different formats. People can write friendly letters, business letters, news articles, advertisements, reports, lists, paragraphs, etc. Creative writing can take on any of these formats and more. Creative writing can be done in straight lines or curves; and the writing can even take the form of an object, such as the object they are describing.

Have students select a format to use. Allow students to select a simple paragraph or a more creative format. Give students more time to write, using their selected formats.

F. Give students a strategy to help them edit their writing.

Teach students that when writing creatively, they do not need to use all of the rules of the English language that they usually use. When they are writing creatively, they will sometimes have the freedom to break rules creatively. Authors usually break rules for a reason, however. For example, authors might want to write the way people speak, they might want to be funny, or they might be trying to make a point.

Rules should be broken the same way throughout the writing. For example, if students choose not to use capital letters or complete sentences, they should continue to "break the rule" throughout the entire piece of writing.

Encourage students to think about why they might want to break a rule and how it might make their writing more interesting. For example, if students are writing about a dictionary, they might choose to misspell words for humor, since a job of a dictionary is to provide correct spellings.

Give students time to edit their papers.

G. Publish students' ideas.

Option 1: Create a booklet with all the students' writing. Give each student a copy of the booklet to keep.

Option 2: Have students select a part of their writing that uses one of the creative-writing tricks. Then, have them read the selection aloud and have the class identify which creative-writing trick was being used.

Common Tricks to Write Creatively

Personification

✳ making something that is not alive act like a human

Write an example: _____

_____

Alliteration

✳ using the same consonant sounds several times

Write an example: _____

_____

Onomatopoeia

✳ words that are spelled the way they sound

Write an example: _____

_____

Metaphor

✳ a comparison (**Note:** don't use the word "like" or "as")

Write an example: _____

_____

Simile

✳ a type of metaphor that uses the word "like" or "as"

Write an example: _____

_____

Imagery

✳ words that tell what something looks like, smells like, feels like, sounds like, or tastes like

Write an example: _____

_____

Hyperbole

✳ a large exaggeration

Write an example: _____

_____

The Reading Assignment

Directions: Read "My Buddy, My Bike" and complete the assignment below.

My Buddy, My Bike

Peddling down a perfect path,

pushing with power, then pausing with pride.

That's how I go on my wonderful ride.

Weaving my way through a big city,

stopping and going, slowing and speeding.

Riding that way has a wonderful feeling.

Gliding through forests on muddy trails,

while moving as fast as a cross-country train.

Feeling like turbulence in a plane.

Huffing and puffing to get more air,

breaks squeaking, gears clicking,

Tires bumping, gears grinding.

My bike, a soldier,

brave and true.

My helmet, my armor, protecting me, too.

Peddling down a perfect path,

"Forever!" I cried.

That's how I go on my wonderful ride.

As you read, look for an example of the following:

✳ Personification _____

✳ Alliteration _____

✳ Onomatopoeia _____

✳ Simile _____

✳ Metaphor _____

✳ Imagery _____

✳ Hyperbole _____

The Writing Assignment

Directions: Write about an object of your choice, using creative tricks that authors use.

Gather Your Ideas

What is your object? _____

Use Creative-Writing Tricks

Personification: Give your object some human traits.

_____

Alliteration: Repeat a consonant sound when writing part of the description.

_____

Onomatopoeia: Have your object make a sound.

_____

Metaphor: Compare your object to something else by saying that your object is the other item.

_____

Simile: Use the word "like" or "as" to compare your object to something else.

_____

Imagery (*pick any three of the following*):

Describe what your objects looks like: _____

Describe sounds that your object can make: _____

Describe what your object might smell like: _____

Describe what your object can taste like: _____

Describe what your object might feel like: _____

Hyperbole: Exaggerate something that your object can do.

_____

Lesson Nine

The Reading Assignment

Teacher Direction: Evaluate the answers to the reading assignment.

Objective	Possible Points	Earned Points
You found examples of personification, alliteration, onomatopoeia, simile, metaphor, imagery, and hyperbole in a poem.		
Total Earned Points:		

The Writing Connection

Teacher Direction: Evaluate the use of literary language.

Objective	Possible Points	Earned Points
You used personification, alliteration, onomatopoeia, simile, metaphor, imagery, and hyperbole.		
You chose how to write your description.		
You used (or broke!) rules the same way all through your creative writing.		
You put effort into the writing process.		
Total Earned Points:		

Additional Teacher Comments: _____

_____

_____

_____

_____

Objectives

Reading

✔ To understand the differences between main characters and minor characters

✔ To identify how and why characters change

✔ To identify and evaluate important actions of characters

✔ To relate to characters personally

Writing

✔ To write a fully-developed character description

✔ To use imagery

✔ To use commas when listing items in a series or separating ideas

Lesson Summary

The students will read a story called "The Dreamer." Then, the students will write an original, fully-developed character description.

Materials Needed

✳ copies of the reading assignment (pages 86–87)

✳ copies of the writing assignment (pages 88–89)

✳ handout or overhead of "Understanding Characters" (page 85)

Part I: The Reading Connection

A. Develop interest in the topic.

Ask: "Were you ever in one place but wished that you were somewhere else?" Have students share their experiences.

B. Encourage students to make predictions about the reading.

Tell the students that they will be reading a story called "The Dreamer." Ask students to make predictions about the story. *Ask:* "Based on the title of the story, what do you think this story might be about?" Allow students to give creative answers.

C. Encourage good reading habits.

Remind students that stories have characters. Some characters are described in great detail; others are described in less detail. Usually, the more important the character is to the story, the more an author will describe the character. Readers need to be able to recognize the important characters in a story so that the reader can focus on them. Distribute (or display on an overhead projector) the student handout entitled "Understanding Characters" (page 85). Review the page with students.

Part I: The Reading Connection *(cont.)*

D. Establish a purpose for reading.

Pass out copies of "The Dreamer" (pages 86–87) for the students to read. Encourage students to focus on the characters in the story. Read aloud the questions that the students should answer as they read the story.

E. Define and extend word meaning.

The word *journal* is used in the story, and it might be a new word for some of the students. Write the word on the board and help students to decode the word. Explain that a journal is a place where people write down their thoughts. One type of journal is a diary.

F. Allow ample time for students to read the story and complete the reading assignment.

G. Discuss the answers to the reading assignment together.

Answers will vary for some of the following questions.

1. *Who is the main character in the story?* Emily P. Slater is the main character in the story.

2. *Who are the two minor characters in the story?* Emily's father and mother are two minor characters in the story.

3. *How does the author describe the main character?* The author describes her long hair, her clothing style (sometimes trendy, sometimes not), and her speech (no particular accent). The author also describes how Emily is feeling. The author explains that Emily feels like she does not belong anywhere and that she is always dreaming about being somewhere that she isn't.

4. *How does the author describe one of the minor characters?* The author briefly describes Emily's father as hard-working and tired at the end of the day. The author briefly describes Emily's mother as working long hours and then bringing more work home to complete at night.

5. *How and why does Emily change in the story?* Emily changes by deciding to keep a journal. She teaches herself to focus on enjoying where she is, instead of focusing on where she is not. She does this to help herself be a happier person.

6. *Is Emily the kind of person you would like to know? Why or why not?* Answers will vary.

7. *Tell why you are like or unlike one of the characters in the story.* Answers will vary.

Part II: The Writing Connection

A. Develop interest in the topic.

On a piece of paper, have students list 10 first names. Then, have them list 10 middle names and then 10 last names. Finally, have students list 10 nicknames that they've heard. Give students an opportunity to share some of the names on their lists.

B. Explain the writing assignment to the students.

Explain to the students that they are going to create a fully-developed character. That means they are going to describe a character in as much detail as possible. The more details that the students are able to provide, the better other people will be able to picture that character.

C. Assist students in organizing their character descriptions.

Hand out copies of the writing assignment (pages 88–89). Guide students through the steps on the writing-assignment handout.

* ✴ Explain that students need to include how the character's life needs to change, how the change happens, and how the character grows.

* ✴ The students should include at least two other elements about their characters in their descriptions, as well.

* ✴ Encourage students to add as many details onto their lists as possible. You might want to remind students that this assignment is a fictional-writing assignment, although they can pull ideas from people that they have met in their lives.

D. Allow writing time.

Once students have gathered their ideas, have students begin putting their ideas into paragraphs. A writing method students can use is to put each organized group of ideas into a separate paragraph. For example, one paragraph might be about what the character looks like and another paragraph might be about the character's life.

Give students ample time to write their paragraphs. As they are working, walk around the room and offer guidance.

Part II: The Writing Connection *(cont.)*

E. Give students a strategy to help them revise their writing.

Explain that writers use the term *imagery* to mean the words that they use when describing something. In order for the students to make their characters fully developed, they will have to use imagery in their writing. *Imagery* is words that describe what things look, feel, sound, smell, and taste like.

Have students see if they can add any more imagery into their writing.

F. Give students a strategy to help them edit their writing.

Remind students to use commas when separating ideas or listing things. Write the following example on the board:

My character has freckles, soft hair scented with strawberry shampoo, and blue-green eyes.

Show students how commas are used in the example to separate the descriptions. Have students check to make sure they did this correctly in their writing. If students do not have any similar sentences in their writing, tell students to add at least one into their writing to show that they can use the skill correctly.

Give students time to edit, using the new skill.

G. Publish students' ideas.

Collect and randomly redistribute the students' character descriptions, making sure that no student gets the description he/she wrote. Have students read their assigned descriptions and draw a sketch of the character.

Hang the pictures around the room. Have each student pick the sketch that they think matches the character they created. Have students discuss why they drew what they did, and have authors discuss how they knew which drawing was their character.

Understanding Characters

Main Characters

* ✳ described with many details

* ✳ important to the story

Minor characters

* ✳ often given common descriptions

* ✳ less important to the story

Once a reader knows that a character is important, the reader can spend time "getting to know" the character by doing the following:

* ✳ creating images of the character in his/her head

* ✳ slowing down when reading descriptions of that character

* ✳ carefully looking at things that the character says and does

* ✳ thinking about why the characters says and does certain things

* ✳ thinking about what the character should and should not do

* ✳ thinking about how and why characters change

* ✳ thinking about what you would do if you were in the story

* ✳ thinking about how you are like or unlike the character

Minor characters are put in a story to interact with the main characters.

Lesson Ten

The Reading Assignment

Directions: Read "The Dreamer" below. Answer the questions that follow on page 87.

The Dreamer

Emily is a common name. But Emily was not a common person. Emily P. Slater grew up half the time with her mother in the big city and the other half of the time with her father on the farm.

Emily had light brown, medium-length hair. She did not have a strong clothing style. She would sometimes look trendy, and other times she just dressed to be comfortable. And when she talked, she did not sound like she was from any one place.

So Emily felt like she did not belong anywhere. When she was on the farm, she missed the city life and the city lights. When she was in the city, she missed the quiet sounds of nature, and the bright stars. Emily spent all her time dreaming that she was somewhere else.

Emily's mother worked long hours and then worked for hours more from home. She did not have the time to notice that something was bothering Emily. Emily's father also worked hard all day and was tired by sundown. He, too, did not notice that something was bothering Emily.

But someone did notice: Emily P. Slater noticed. She decided that she was tired of always dreaming of being somewhere else. She wanted her life to be different. She knew that only she could change how she was feeling. But how could she make the change? She knew that she could not move her father to the city or her mother to the farm. Plus, she did not want to give up either farm-life or city-life. So, she thought and thought.

Finally, Emily decided that her life did not need to change at all. She realized how lucky she was to be able to have two wonderful kinds of lives. What she needed to change was her thinking. Instead of missing a place where she was not, she needed to start enjoying where she was.

So, Emily P. Slater decided to keep a journal. Every day, she would write about what she enjoyed about where she was that day. And her plan worked. She trained herself to think about what made her happy at the moment, instead of always dreaming. Well, sometimes, that is. She still dreamed about . . .

The Reading Assignment *(cont.)*

Answer the following questions:

1. Who is the main character in the story? _____

2. Who are the two minor characters in the story? _____

   _____

3. How does the author describe the main character? _____

   _____

   _____

4. How does the author describe one the minor characters? _____

   _____

5. How and why does Emily change in the story? _____

   _____

   _____

6. Is Emily the kind of person you would like to know? Why or why not? _____

   _____

   _____

   _____

7. Tell why you are like or unlike one of the characters in the story. _____

   _____

   _____

   _____

The Writing Assignment

Directions: Create a fully-developed character.

Step One (*Describe your character.*)

Name Your Character: _____

Describe what your character looks like. What does this person look like? How does this person dress? How does this person walk?

_____   _____

_____   _____

_____   _____

_____   _____

Describe what your character sounds like. How does this person talk? What other sounds can describe this person?

_____   _____

_____   _____

_____   _____

_____   _____

Describe what your character is like. What is the person like? What does this person like to do? What things are important to this person? What things are not important to this person?

_____   _____

_____   _____

_____   _____

_____   _____

Lesson Ten

The Writing Assignment *(cont.)*

Describe your character's life. Where does your character live? How does your character live? What does your character do?

_____   _____

_____   _____

_____   _____

_____   _____

List other interesting descriptions that you can think of to describe your character.

_____   _____

_____   _____

_____   _____

_____   _____

Step Two (*Show how your character grows as a person.*)

What about your character's life needs to change?

_____

_____

_____

_____

How does the change happen?

_____

_____

_____

_____

How does your character grow as a result of the change?

_____

_____

_____

_____

Lesson
Ten

The Reading Assignment

Teacher Direction: Evaluate the answers to the reading questions.

Objective	Possible Points	Earned Points
You identify major and minor characters.		
You identify descriptions the author gives of different characters.		
You identify how and why a character changes.		
You can evaluate and relate to a character in the story.		
Total Earned Points:		

The Writing Assignment

Directions: Evaluate the character description.

Objective	Possible Points	Earned Points
You attempted to create a character that was fully developed.		
You organized your ideas.		
You used imagery in your writing.		
You used commas when listing, or to separate ideas.		
You put effort into using the writing process.		
Total Earned Points:		

Additional Teacher Comments: _____

_____

Lesson Eleven

Objectives

Reading

✔ To identify the five parts of a story's plot: introduction, rising action, climax, falling action, and conclusion

Writing

✔ To write the falling action and conclusion to a given story

✔ To add details to a story as a revision strategy

✔ To use capital letters correctly

Lesson Summary

The students will read a story called "One Step at a Time" and identify different parts of the story's plot. Then, students will write the ending of a story called "A Not-So-Fun Park."

Materials Needed

✶ copies of the reading assignment (pages 94–95)

✶ copies of the writing assignment (pages 96–97)

Part I: The Reading Connection

A. Develop interest in the topic.

Ask: "If you could go somewhere that you've never been, where would you choose to go and why?" Answers will vary.

B. Encourage students to make predictions about the reading.

Tell the students that they will be reading a story called "One Step at a Time." *Ask:* "Based on the title of the story, what do you think this story might be about?" Allow students to give creative answers.

C. Encourage good reading habits.

Tell students that plot is the movement of a story from the beginning to the end. Understanding how a story is told helps readers follow the story as they are reading it. There are five basic parts of a story's plot:

1. *Introduction:* Readers are told who the story is about and when and where the story takes place.

2. *Rising Action:* The problem is told.

3. *Climax:* The problem grows bigger, and it must be addressed.

4. *Falling Action:* The problem begins to reach an end.

5. *Conclusion:* The problem is ended.

(**Note:** Point out that not all stories have all five of these parts.)

Part I: The Reading Connection *(cont.)*

D. Establish a purpose for reading.

Distribute copies of the reading assignment (pages 94–95). Tell the students that as they read they should look for the five different parts of the plot. Read aloud the instructions that are on the handout.

E. Define and extend word meaning.

The word *spectacular* appears in the story, and it might be a new word for the students. Explain that *spectacular* means "amazing" or "something worth looking at."

Extend word understanding by pointing out that another word for *eyeglasses* is *spectacles*. Students should connect the word *look* to the words *spectacular* and *spectacles*. In Latin, *spec* means "look or see."

F. Allow ample time for students to read the story and complete the reading assignment.

G. Discuss the answers to the reading assignment together.

1. *Circle the* **introduction**. The introduction of this story is in the first three paragraphs, where Samantha's home and family life are described.

2. *Put a question mark near the* **rising action**. The rising action in this story is presented in the forth paragraph. Samantha feels as if she is the last to do everything, and she wants to be the first in her family to climb a mountain. However, her father does not think she is ready.

3. *Put an exclamation mark near the* **climax**. The climax of the story is in paragraphs five and six. Samantha decides that she is going to prove to her father that she is ready to climb a mountain, and her father finally sees that she is ready.

4. *Put a down arrow near the* **falling action**. The falling action of the story begins in paragraph seven. Samantha and her father climb the mountain and experience many firsts together.

5. *Draw a smiley face at the* **conclusion**. The conclusion occurs in the last three paragraphs. Samantha reaches the top of the mountain.

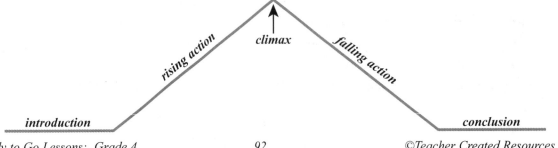

Part II: The Writing Connection

A. Develop interest in the topic.

Ask: "What experiences have you had at a fair, carnival, or fun park?" Allow students time to share their experiences.

B. Explain the writing assignment to the students.

Tell the students that they will be reading part of a story about two boys who go to an amusement park together to ride some roller coasters. Tell the students that the story stops in the middle after the rising action (problem) has been presented. The students will write the climax, falling action, and conclusion of the story.

C. Assist students in organizing their ideas.

1. Hand out copies of the writing assignment on pages 96–97. Give students time to read the story entitled "A Not-So-Fun Park."

2. Put students in small groups to discuss possible endings to the story.

3. Regroup as a class. Have students share some of their ideas as you jot down ideas on the board.

D. Allow writing time.

Give students ample time to write their own endings to the story. As they are working, walk around the room offering guidance.

E. Give students a strategy to help them revise their writing.

Tell students that details are what make stories interesting. Encourage the students to go back to the original story and add details, like names of theme parks or specific rides, descriptions of the boys, etc. Not only will this make the story more interesting, but it will make the story more original.

F. Give students a strategy to help them edit their writing.

Remind students that names are capitalized. Names of people, places, and specific rides are capitalized. Names of general rides, like roller coasters, are not capitalized.

Have the students check to see that they used correct capitalization in their stories.

G. Publish students' ideas.

Option 1: Select some particularly unique versions of the story to read aloud to the class.

Option 2: Have the students select their favorite part of their stories to share with the class.

The Reading Assignment

Directions: Read "One Step at a Time" below and on page 95. Follow the instructions on page 95.

One Step at a Time

Samantha lived where it was flat. Very flat. Understand, she loved where she lived. She loved seeing the corn poking out of the ground in the spring, growing taller and taller as the days got longer and longer. She loved getting lost in the stalks as the corn grew taller than she. Then, as the air chilled, everything turned brown and was cut down, and she loved being able to see for miles and miles.

Samantha dreamed of mountains, though. She dreamed of climbing high above the corn and high into the clouds.

Samantha was born into a family with five children. Saul, Ceil, Sammy, and Candice were all older than she was. Saul was the first born. Ceil was the first to talk. Sammy was the first to get on a sports team, and Candice was the first to play an instrument well. Samantha always felt like she was the last.

Every year she would ask her dad if he would take her to the mountains. Every year he gave the same reply: "Not this year, Samantha. You are still too young." But this year, Samantha was determined. She wanted to go to the mountains. She wanted to be the first in her family to climb to the top of a mountain.

This year, she was not going to *ask* her father if she was ready, she was going to *prove* to her father that she was ready. So, she worked alongside her father all day in the fields all summer long. As long as he was at work, she was at work.

One day, her father turned to her and said, "Samantha, I think you are ready. This year, we will go to the mountains. We'll see how far you get."

Lesson
Eleven

The Reading Assignment

One Step at a Time *(cont.)*

The oldest male in the family and the youngest female in the family set off together to climb a mountain. As they climbed, they pointed out things to each other. They both saw a bear up in a tree for the first time. They both saw some young boys fly fishing by the stream for the first time. They both saw snow in the summer for the first time.

Samantha was starting to get tired. They had walked so far already. But her father said, "You can do it, Samantha. I know you can. Let's rest and eat and then continue."

After a bite and a rest, Samantha felt better, so they continued up. A few hours later, they reached the top.

Samantha was used to seeing far when the ground was flat, but she had not known how far it was possible to see from the top of a mountain. She thought that perhaps she could see forever. It was spectacular.

Father and daughter climbed down the mountain together. Perhaps this was the first mountain that they had climbed together, but it would certainly not be the last.

As you read the story, do the following:

1. Circle the *introduction*.

   The introduction tells who the story is about, and when and where the story takes place.

2. Put a question mark (**?**) near the *rising action*.

   The rising action is the growing problem in the story.

3. Put an exclamation mark (**!**) near the *climax*.

   At the climax, something happens to stop the problem from growing bigger.

4. Put a down arrow (↓) near the *falling action*.

   During the falling action, the problem begins to come to an end.

5. Draw a smiley face (☺) at the *conclusion*.

   Here, the problem ends.

Lesson
Eleven

The Writing Assignment

Directions: Finish the story by adding the falling action and the conclusion. Begin by writing your name on the blank line.

A Not-So-Fun Park

by Jessica Kissel and _____

    Jacob and Adam had been looking forward to this outing for weeks. They were going to an amusement park hours from home. They had been there years ago, but they were not tall enough then to ride any of the coasters. This year, they were tall enough—and they were ready to ride them!

    Jacob's parents dropped them off at the park early in the morning and explained that they would pick up the two boys at the end of the day.

    It was hot out, but Jacob and Adam were too excited to mind the heat. They also did not mind the crowds in their excitement.

    Suddenly, Adam turned to say something to Jacob but could not find him anywhere. He looked around, called Jacob's name, and even stood on a high bench to look down into the crowds. They were separated and lost.

Now write the <u>climax</u> of the story. What happened next? When and how do the two boys find each other? After writing the climax, complete the story on page 97.

_____

_____

_____

_____

_____

_____

_____

Lesson
Eleven

The Writing Assignment *(cont.)*

Directions: Finish the story by adding the falling action and the conclusion.

Write the <u>falling action</u> of the story. What happens next?
What, if anything, do the boys do to try to fix their day?

_____

_____

_____

_____

_____

_____

_____

_____

_____

Write the <u>conclusion</u> of the story. How does the story end?

_____

_____

_____

_____

_____

_____

_____

_____

_____

The Reading Assignment

Teacher Direction: Evaluate the answers to the reading assignment.

Objective	Possible Points	Earned Points
You found the different parts of the story's plot.		
Total Earned Points:		

The Writing Connection

Teacher Direction: Evaluate the original story ending.

Objective	Possible Points	Earned Points
You wrote the climax for your story.		
You wrote the falling action for your story.		
You wrote an ending for your story.		
You added details into your story.		
You capitalized words correctly.		
You put effort into the writing process.		
Total Earned Points:		

Additional Teacher Comments: _____

_____

_____

_____

Lesson
Twelve

Objectives

Reading

✔ To identify compare/contrast, problem/solution, idea/support, cause/effect, and time-order patterns that textbooks use to present information

Writing

✔ To write paragraphs using compare/contrast, problem/solution, idea/support, cause/effect, and time-order patterns

✔ To use key words while writing to make writing more clear

✔ To spell words correctly

Lesson Summary

The students will read sample passages and identify informational patterns that textbooks use to present information. (Students will select from compare/contrast, problem/solution, idea/support, cause/effect, and time order.) Then, the students will write their own passages, using those same patterns.

(**Note:** Lesson Eight also focuses on these same patterns, but Lesson Eight does not specifically focus on how these patterns are used in textbooks. Lesson Eight provides a more general overview of how authors and readers can use these patterns.)

Materials Needed

✶ copies of the reading assignmenst (pages 103–105)

✶ copies of the writing assignment (page 106)

✶ handouts (or overhead) of "Common Ways Textbooks Tell Information" (page 102)

✶ dictionaries

Part I: The Reading Connection

A. Develop interest in the topic.

Ask the following questions. Student answers will vary.

✶ "How many textbooks do you have?"

✶ "What kinds of textbooks do you have?"

✶ "What kinds of textbooks do you *not* have, but other people might have?"

✶ "How is a textbook different from other types of books?"

Part I: The Reading Connection *(cont.)*

B. Encourage students to make predictions about the reading.

Tell the students that the goal of a textbook is to teach information to readers. Textbooks use specific ways to tell information to readers so that readers can better understand what is trying to be taught.

Ask students to predict different ways that information is presented in textbooks. Have them think about textbooks they have read and how information is presented to them in those textbooks. Answers will vary but might include that textbooks use illustrations to help explain things, that information is presented in a specific order, that questions are asked and then answered, that students are asked to try things on their own, etc.

C. Encourage good reading habits.

Hand out copies of (or display on an overhead) page 102. Explain to students that in this lesson they will be focusing on five different ways that textbooks tell information to their readers. Review with the students those five ways:

1. **Compare and Contrast**—Textbooks show how things are the same and how they differ.

2. **Time Order**—Textbooks tell things in the order that they happened or will happen.

3. **Cause and Effect**—Textbooks tell how or why something happened or will happen.

4. **Idea and Support**—Textbooks tell an idea and then explain the idea.

5. **Problem and Solution**—Textbooks tell a problem and then tell how to solve the problem or how the problem was solved.

D. Establish a purpose for reading.

Distribute copies of pages 103–105. Tell students that they will be reading five different passages. Each passage will be about pumpkins, but each will present information in a different way. Students should try to identify which way each passage is using to tell information: compare/contrast, time order, cause/effect, idea/support, or problem/solution.

E. Define and extend word meaning.

Students might have trouble reading the word *competition*. Write the word on the board and help the students to decode the word. Point out that the word has a common /tion/ ending. Students may recognize that the word *compete* is related to *competition*. A competition is a contest between two or more people.

F. Allow ample time for students to read the passages and complete the reading assignment.

Part I: The Reading Connection *(cont.)*

G. Discuss the answers to the reading assignment together.

Passage One	Passage Two	Passage Three	Passage Four	Passage Five
cause and effect	*time order*	*compare and contrast*	*problem and solution*	*idea and support*

Part II: The Writing Connection

A. Develop interest in the topic.

Ask: "What do you know about city life?" List the students' responses on the board or overhead. Answers will vary. Sample answers are provided on page 106.

B. Explain the writing assignment to the students.

Distribute copies of the writing assignment (page 106). Explain that information in textbooks is often written in special ways. It is common for textbooks to tell information using the following patterns:

✻ Compare/Contrast   ✻ Cause/Effect   ✻ Idea/Support

✻ Time Order   ✻ Problem/Solution

Tell the students that they will be writing paragraphs using the different ways to tell information. Have students select any four to complete.

C. Allow writing time.

As students are working, walk around the room and offer guidance.

D. Give students a strategy to help them revise their writing.

To make writing more clear, students might want to use specific words to show readers which patterns they are using. Students could include words and phrases such as *in comparison; in contrast; first, second, after that* (i.e., time-order words); *cause; effect; idea; support; reason; problem;* and *solution.*

E. Give students a strategy to help them edit their writing.

Remind students that words that they don't use often are sometimes hard to spell. Encourage students to locate words they are not sure how to spell and to use a dictionary or other source to locate the correct spelling of the word. Give students time to edit.

F. Publish students' ideas.

Have students tear a piece of paper up into five strips. Have them label each paper: *Compare/ Contrast, Time Order, Cause/Effect, Idea/Support,* and *Problem/Solution.*

Read some of the students' paragraphs aloud. Have the students hold up the strip of paper that they feel best describes how the paragraph was written.

Lesson
Twelve

Common Ways Textbooks Tell Information

1. Compare and Contrast

Textbooks show how things are the same and how things are different.

2. Time Order

Textbooks tell things in the order that they happened or will happen.

3. Cause and Effect

Textbooks explain that when one thing happens, it makes something else happen, as well.

4. Idea and Support

Textbooks tell an idea and then explain the idea.

5. Problem and Solution

Textbooks tell a problem and then tell either how to solve it or how it was already solved.

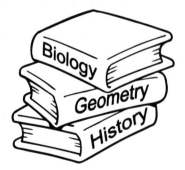

Lesson
Twelve

The Reading Assignment

Directions: Read the five passages below. Then, decide which passage was telling information using:

* ✳ Idea and Support
* ✳ Compare and Contrast
* ✳ Time Order

* ✳ Cause and Effect
* ✳ Problem and Solution

Passage One

With enough water and plenty of room, many people have luck growing pumpkins. But, even the best pumpkin growers can end up with a poor pumpkin patch. Frost can hurt pumpkin plants. Young pumpkin plants have trouble living through a frost. Wind can also hurt a pumpkin patch. Strong winds can hurt the pumpkin vines. Animals and insects can also hurt the pumpkin plant. Gophers, moles and beetles can damage pumpkin plants by digging them up, or bruising them. Many people have a great time growing pumpkins, but there are some things that can cause a pumpkin patch to decline.

How did this passage tell information? _____

_____

_____

Passage Two

There are certain steps that should be followed when growing pumpkins. First, wait until the weather reaches 70 degrees, and the frost season is over. Then, soak the seeds overnight. Space the seeds 6–8 inches in the ground and cover them with an inch of dirt. After that, water the seeds carefully. Wait about 125 days, watching the plants for watering needs or other problems. Then, pick your pumpkins!

How did this passage tell information? _____

_____

_____

Lesson Twelve

The Reading Assignment *(cont.)*

Passage Three

There are many different types of pumpkin to choose from. The Baby Bear weighs between 2 and 5 pounds. It is small and flat. The Small Sugar is the same size as the Baby Bear, but it is better to use for making pies.

The Ghost Rider is dark orange and weighs between 15 and 25 pounds. It has a green stem on it. The Pankow's Field weighs the same as the Ghost Rider, but it is known for its very tall handles.

The orange Atlantic Giant can grow to be very large. They often grow to be 50 to 100 pounds. The Munchkin, also an orange pumpkin, is one of the smallest pumpkins there is.

How did this passage tell information? _____

_____

_____

The Reading Assignment *(cont.)*

Passage Four

There was a pumpkin-carving competition in town, and Albert wanted to win. He spent hours carving many different pumpkins. He carved words into pumpkins, witches on brooms, and scary faces. But Albert could only put one of the pumpkins into the competition. He did not know which one to pick. Suddenly, Albert had an idea: he decided to hold his own pumpkin competition. He invited his friends and family over to see all of his pumpkins. They all voted on their favorites. A pumpkin with a scary face won. So, Albert put that one into the town's competition.

How did this passage tell information? _____

_____

_____

Passage Five

When looking for something useful to grow, pumpkins are a good choice. There are many different uses for pumpkins. Pumpkins can be made into soup, served as a side dish for dinner, turned into pumpkin butter, or used to make pies and breads. Pumpkins can also be used for decoration.

How did this passage tell information? _____

_____

_____

The Writing Assignment

Use the information below to write passages that could be found in a textbook about cities. Use four out of five of the writing patterns that were taught in class.

Writing Patterns

* Idea and Support
* Compare and Contrast
* Time Order
* Cause and Effect
* Problem and Solution

Information About Cities

* There are many different types of people who live in cities.

* Buses, subways, trains, and taxis make it easy to get around in cities.

* There are many different types of restaurants to choose from in big cities.

* Cities have problems such as crime and pollution.

* Cities often are in need of money to deal with problems.

* Cities attract tourists.

* There are many things to do in cities, such as sightseeing, visiting museums, watching plays, listening to music, hanging out in coffee shops or bookstores, taking classes, and eating at restaurants.

* There are a lot of different jobs in cities.

The Reading Assignment

Teacher Direction: Evaluate the answers to the reading assignment.

Objective	Possible Points	Earned Points
You found the different parts of the story's plot.		
	Total Earned Points:	

The Writing Connection

Teacher Direction: Evaluate the answers to the writing assignment.

Objective	Possible Points	Earned Points
You wrote information in different ways: compare/contrast, problem/solution, time order, cause/effect, and idea/support.		
You used words to help the reader figure out what pattern you were using to tell information.		
You put effort into spelling words correctly.		
You put effort into the writing process.		
	Total Earned Points:	

Additional Teacher Comments: _____

_____

_____

_____

_____

Lesson Thirteen

Objectives

Reading

✔ To vary speeds of reading when reading for different purposes

Writing

✔ To write paragraphs describing personal reading habits

✔ To use topic sentences

✔ To identify and edit run-on sentences

Lesson Summary

The students will read an article called "Double Time." Students will practice skimming, skipping, and rereading information when needed. Then, students will write paragraphs that describe their own reading habits.

Materials

✷ copies of the reading assignment (pages 112–114)

✷ copies of the writing assignment (pages 115–116)

Part I: The Reading Connection

A. Develop interest in the topic.

Open up a discussion about twins. *Ask questions such as:* "If you had to recommend names for a pair of twins, what names would you choose and why? What do you know about twins? Have you ever met any twins?"

B. Encourage students to make predictions about the reading.

Tell the students that they will be reading an informational article called "Double Time." *Ask:* "Based on the title of the article, what do you think this article might be about?" Allow students to give reasonable answers. Point out that the article is an informational article. Ask the students what type of information they think might be provided in it.

C. Encourage good reading habits.

Teach students that everyone has different speeds of reading. Sometimes, readers read very fast in order to get the idea of what is written or to find specific information. This is called *skimming.* When a person skims, the reader is not really reading every word. *Ask:* "When have you skimmed something?" Answers will vary.

Sometimes, readers read so fast that they skip a full sentence or even more. This is called *skipping. Ask:* "When have you skipped something?" Answers will vary.

Readers also *reread* information that is very important or hard to understand. *Ask:* "When have you reread something?" Answers will vary.

Lesson
Thirteen

Part I: The Reading Connection *(cont.)*

C. Encourage good reading habits. *(cont.)*

Students are often asked to read for information in their classes. When asked to read for information, students should change their speed of reading depending what they are reading.

* ✸ Readers can *skim* to find the information that they need or to get an idea of what was written.

* ✸ Readers can *skip* over information that they do not need.

* ✸ Readers should slow down when they find the information that they need and *reread* when they need to do so.

D. Establish a purpose for reading.

Explain to the students that they will practice the skills of skimming, skipping, and rereading. Pass out copies of the reading assignment (pages 112–114). Read the directions aloud to the students.

E. Define and extend word meaning.

The word *gender* is used in the article. Students may not be familiar with this word. Write the word on the board so students can see how to spell it, and learn to read the word. Point out that the letter *g* in this word makes a soft /j/ sound. One's gender is either male or female.

gender

F. Allow ample time for students to read the article and complete the reading assignment.

G. Discuss the answers to the reading assignment together.

1. *Skim the article to find out why twins might not share the same birthday. How long did it take you to find the information?* Answers will vary. *Why might twins not share the same birthday?* Twins won't share a birthday when one twin is born very late in the day and the other twin is born early the next day.

2. *Read the first paragraph. What is one difference between identical and fraternal twins?* Answers might vary. One difference between identical and fraternal twins is that identical twins are created from one egg, and fraternal twins are created from two eggs. *How did you read that paragraph? Did you skim it, skip it, read it carefully, or reread it? Why?* Answers will vary, but most students would have slowed down or even reread that paragraph.

Part I: The Reading Connection *(cont.)*

G. Discuss the answers to the reading assignment together. *(cont.)*

3. *Skim the article again. Find out why twins attract a lot of attention. How long did it take you to find the information?* Answers will vary. *What is one reason that twins attract a lot of attention?* Answers might vary. One reason twins attract a lot of attention is that twins are not that common.

4. *Now re-read the article "Double Time." Are there any parts of the article you chose to skip? Why?* Answers will vary. There are parts of the article that students did not need to read to answer the questions. The students might have opted to skip those paragraphs.

Part II: The Writing Connection

A. Develop interest in the topic.

Write three columns on the board. Label the columns as follows: ***Slow***, ***Skim***, and ***Skip***.

1. Ask the students to list things that they read slowly. Write their responses on the board. Encourage answers such as descriptions of main characters or setting, dialogue, directions, definitions, information they need for classes, notes from friends, lists from parents, etc.

2. Ask the students to list things that they skim (i.e., searching for specific information). Write their responses on the board. Encourage answers such as news articles, textbooks to find information that they need, long descriptions in books, computer websites, etc.

3. Ask the students to list things that they skip as they read (i.e., things that are not important and not interesting). Write their responses on the board. Encourage answers such as something they already know, something that is boring, etc.

B. Explain the writing assignment to the students.

Tell the students that they will be thinking about their own reading patterns and answering the following questions:

1. What types of things do you read slowly and carefully?

2. What types of things do you skim as you read?

3. When do you skip things as you read?

4. How can you be a better reader by changing the speeds at which you read different things?

Remind students that all readers change their speed of reading as they read. Explain that as readers, they should be aware that they need to read some things slowly, skim other things, and skip some things completely.

This activity can be completed at several times throughout the year. As students' reading skills develop and as their interests change, they will find that their reading styles change, too. Students should actively think about how they read and how they can become better readers.

Part II: The Writing Connection *(cont.)*

C. Assist students in organizing their answers.

Hand out the writing assignment on pages 115–116. Using the ideas on the board and adding ideas of their own, students should fill out the chart on page 116 so that the answers apply to their individual reading habits. Encourage students to really think about how they read.

D. Allow writing time.

Give students ample time to answer the questions om page 115 in the form of paragraphs. As the students are working, walk around the room and offer guidance.

E. Give students a strategy to help them revise their writing.

Explain that a good paragraph starts with a topic sentence. A *topic sentence* is a sentence that tells readers what information is going to be in the paragraph. With the students, discuss possible topic sentences for the paragraphs that they are writing. Answers could include:

1. There are many different things that I read slowly and carefully.
   I read certain things slowly and carefully.

2. There are many different things that I skim as I read.
   As I read, there are some things that I skim.

3. There are many things that I skip as I read.
   Sometimes I skip things as I read.

4. There are some things that I can change so that I can become a better reader.
   I am going to try some things differently so that I can be a stronger reader.

Give students time to revise, using the new skill.

F. Give students a strategy to help them edit their writing.

Remind students that as they edit, they should look for *run-on sentences*. Run-on sentences are sentences that have more than one sentence inside of them. Share this example of a run-on sentence:

✸ *I skim when I am looking for information I skim when I am trying to answer a question.*

Have students look in their paragraphs to try to find examples of run-on sentences. Then, show students two ways to edit the incorrect sentence. One way is to split the sentence up into two sentences, and the other way is to add a comma and a connecting word.

✸ *I skim when I am looking for information. I skim when I am trying to answer a question.*

✸ *I skim when I am looking for information, and I skim when I am trying to answer a question.*

Give students time to search for run-on sentences in their own writing.

G. Publish students' ideas.

Have students select which paragraph they feel is their best writing sample. Have students share their paragraph with a partner or the class. Have students discuss why they feel the paragraph was written well.

The Reading Assignment

Directions: Read "Double Time" below and on page 113. Answer the questions that follow on page 114.

Double Time

When two babies are born around the same time (from the same mother), the babies are called twins. There are two different kinds of twins. Identical twins are made when the mother's egg splits into two eggs. Identical twins often look the same. Identical twins are always the same gender. Fraternal twins are made from two different eggs. Fraternal twins may look alike, but they can also look very different from each other. Fraternal twins can be the same gender, but they don't have to be.

Most twins share the same birthday, but not all of them do. Sometimes one twin is born late on one day, and the other twin is born early the next morning.

Twins must learn to share very early on in their lives. To begin with, they share space in their mother's womb. Later, they must also share the time and attention of the people taking care of them. They often share many of their toys. But twins do not share everything. Many twins grow to have different interests, and they often learn to do new things at different times.

Today, most people who have twins know that they are going to be having twins before the twins are born. But not too long ago, that was not the case. Imagine the surprise when people thought they were having one baby, but they had two instead!

Some people like to give twins similar names, such as Molly and Polly. Other people like to give twins very different names. Some people like to dress twins the same, others like to dress them similarly, and others like to dress their twins differently. When twins grow older, though, they often have their own tastes and styles of clothing.

Twins often attract a lot of attention. Perhaps this is because twins are not so common. Also, people who are not a twin may wonder what life would be like to have a twin.

The Reading Assignment *(cont.)*

Double Time *(cont.)*

Every year in Twinsburg, Ohio, there is a festival just for twins. There are competitions for the most similar-looking twins, talent shows, and other events for families who attend.

There are a lot of groups that have formed to help give information to people with twins. Some of these groups meet with the parents and twins, some groups have meeting just for the parents, and other groups have meetings just for twins.

When people see twins, they often say things like, "Oh, double trouble!" But other people see twins as a double blessing. Most parents of twins will agree that twins are a lot of work—but well worth the effort.

Lesson
Thirteen

The Reading Assignment *(cont.)*

Directions: Follow these directions to answer questions about the informational article "Double Time."

1. Skim the article to find out why twins might not share the same birthday. How long did it take you to find the information? _____

   Why might twins not share the same birthday? _____

   _____

2. Read the first paragraph. What is one difference between identical and fraternal twins?

   _____

   _____

   How did you read that paragraph? Did you skim it, skip it, read it carefully, or reread it? Why?

   _____

   _____

3. Skim the article again. Find out why twins attract a lot of attention. How long did it take you to find the information? _____

   What is one reason that twins attract a lot of attention? _____

   _____

4. Now, re-read "Double Time." Are there any parts of the article you chose to skip? Why?

   _____

   _____

The Writing Assignment

Directions: Answer the following questions by writing paragraphs explaining how you read.

1. **What types of things do you read slowly and carefully?**

2. **What types of things do you skim as you read?**

3. **When do you skip things as you read?**

4. **How can you become a better reader?**

Lesson Thirteen

The Writing Assignment *(cont.)*

Directions: Fill out the chart below to explain how you vary your reading rates.

I Slowly Read	I Skim	I Skip

The Reading Assignment

Teacher Direction: Evaluate the answers to the reading assignment.

Objective	Possible Points	Earned Points
You tried to vary your speed as you read the informational article.		
Total Earned Points:		

The Writing Connection

Teacher Direction: Evaluate the answers to the writing assignment.

Objective	Possible Points	Earned Points
You described your reading habits.		
You found a way to try to improve as a reader.		
You used topic sentences.		
You avoided run-on sentences.		
You put effort into using the writing process effectively.		
Total Earned Points:		

Additional Teacher Comments: _____

_____

_____

_____

_____

Objectives

Reading

✔ To make and revise predictions while reading

Writing

✔ To write an original story that encourages readers to make predictions

✔ To use different types of sentences while writing by adding imperative sentences

Lesson Summary

The students will read "Unusual" and make and revise predictions as they read the story. Then, the students will write original stories that encourage other readers to make predictions.

Materials Needed

✴ copies of the reading assignment (pages 122–123)

✴ copies of the writing assignment (page 124)

Part I: The Reading Connection

A. Develop interest in the topic.

Ask: "Guess what we are going to do today?" Encourage students to make realistic guesses based on what they know about the class.

B. Encourage students to make predictions about the reading.

Explain that we always make guesses about what is going to happen to us in our own lives. We might make guesses about what we will do in the afternoon or at the mall or on vacation.

Readers should always make guesses while they are reading, too. These guesses are called *predictions*. Readers need to think about what they are reading and make guesses about what will happen next based on their own experiences and clues that are given in the story.

Tell the students that they will be reading a story called "Unusual." Ask students to make predictions about the story. *Ask:* "Based on the title of the story, what do you think this story might be about?" Allow students to give creative answers.

Part I: The Reading Connection *(cont.)*

C. Encourage good reading habits.

Ask students to think about their own reading habits. Have them think about whether or not they make predictions, or guesses, as they read. Ask students to discuss what types of predictions readers can make. Answers will vary but should be similar to the following:

* ✳ What is going to happen next?

* ✳ What should a character do or say?

* ✳ What might happen if a character does or says something?

* ✳ What could have happened if a character did or said something differently?

Remind students that sometimes readers make predictions that are right, and sometimes they make predictions that are wrong. Explain to the students that if they make a wrong prediction that does not mean that they are a bad reader. Good readers realize that sometimes predictions are right and sometimes they are wrong. Good readers constantly change their predictions as they get more information.

D. Establish a purpose for reading.

Hand out copies of "Unusual" (pages 122–123) for the students to read. Explain to the students that as they read the story, they will be asked to predict what might happen next. They should write their predictions in the space provided.

This story is divided into sections to encourage students to make predictions. After copying the story, cut it apart into the different sections and distribute each section only after the students have made their predictions.

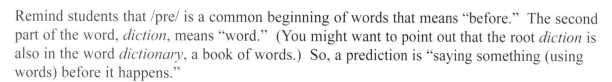

E. Define and extend word meaning.

Remind the students that the word *prediction* means "guess." Write the word on the board. Break up the word for the students: pre•diction.

Remind students that /pre/ is a common beginning of words that means "before." The second part of the word, *diction*, means "word." (You might want to point out that the root *diction* is also in the word *dictionary*, a book of words.) So, a prediction is "saying something (using words) before it happens."

F. Allow ample time for students to read the story and complete the reading assignment.

Part I: The Reading Connection *(cont.)*

G. Discuss the answers to the reading assignment together.

Answers will vary. Allow students time to share predictions that they made that were correct and incorrect, but encourage students to justify why they made the prediction that they did. v

Part II: The Writing Connection

A. Develop interest in the topic.

Ask the students if they ever made a guess about something that was going to happen in a story, movie, or television show. Have students share their experiences.

B. Explain the writing assignment to the students.

Tell the students that they will try to write a story that gets readers to make guesses about what will happen next in their stories. Distribute copies of page 124. Read the assignment aloud to the students.

C. Assist students in organizing their stories.

Read aloud the first question on the writing-assignment handout. As a class, create a list of ways that authors get readers to make predictions.

How do authors get readers to make predictions? Answers may vary.

* Authors add suspense. (For example, "There was a noise in the hallway." This encourages readers to wonder what the noise is.)

* Authors ask questions. (For example, "Why?" This encourages readers to wonder what the answer to a question might be.)

* Authors don't give all the information at once. (This gets the reader to think about the missing facts.)

* Authors select events that are familiar to people. (This gets readers to think about their own experiences and make guesses based on them.)

* Authors leave clues. (This challenges readers to try to figure out what is going to happen.)

* Authors select titles that give a very small piece of information about a story. (This causes readers to think about why the title was chosen.)

* Authors add pictures to their stories. (Readers can use pictures to make predictions.)

What main events will happen in your story? Encourage students to come up with a simple plot for their story. Encourage students to think about different genres (such as fantasy, mythology, historical fiction, mystery, or biography) to help them to come up with some ideas for their stories.

Lesson Fourteen

Part II: The Writing Connection *(cont.)*

C. Assist students in organizing their stories. *(cont.)*

How will you try to get readers to make predictions as they read your story?

* Have students try some of the suggestions listed in class, or other techniques, to get their readers to want to make predictions.

* Have students add in the question "What do you predict happens next?" to show where they want their readers to make a prediction. (These questions will also be used when students share their stories later on in the lesson.) Students should ask the question "What do you predict happens next?" at least two times within their story.

D. Allow writing time.

Give students ample time to write their stories. As they are working, walk around the room and offer guidance.

E. Explain the writing assignment to the students.

Remind students that there are different types of telling sentences.

* Most sentences make some sort of a statement and have a basic subject/verb structure. These sentences are called *declarative sentences*.

  Example: I gave the dog some water.

* Another type of a sentence makes a command. These type of sentences are called *imperative sentences*. This type of sentence could get a reader thinking about why a command was given and what might happen next in a story.

  Example: Be careful out there.

Encourage students to add at least one imperative sentence to their story. Give students time to revise their writing.

F. Give student a strategy to help them edit their writing.

Remind the students that different type of sentences need different types of punctuation. Most sentences end in a period. However, sentences that are making a strong point might end in an exclamation point, and sentences that ask a question should end in a questin mark.

Have students check to see that they carefully selected their ending punctuation marks to fit different types of sentences. Give students time to edit, using the new skill.

G. Publish students' ideas.

Pair up students and have them read each other's stories and make predictions as they read each other's stories. Lead a discussion about what authors did to encourage readers to make predictions.

The Reading Assignment

Directions: Read "Unusual" below and on page 123. Make predictions as you read.

Unusual

I had a usual day at school. Nothing out of the ordinary happened. I had the usual Wednesday lunch of chicken nuggets and fries. I had the usual classes, and I had the usual load of homework to finish.

But when I got home, I found out some unusual news. "Guess what?" my father asked.

Make a prediction. What will happen next in the story?

_____

_____

_____

✂ —

"What?" I asked, mystified.

"We're moving," my father answered.

"Oh," I said. I had heard better news. I was sad. Disappointed. Angry. Confused. I felt a lot of other emotions, too. I dropped my book bag without saying another word and ran to my room. Soon, there was a knock on the door.

Was your last prediction right? Why or why not?

_____

_____

_____

Make a prediction. What will happen next in the story?

_____

_____

_____

The Reading Assignment *(cont.)*

Unusual *(cont.)*

It was my father. "Are you okay?" he asked. "You did not let me finish. You did not even ask me where we were going."

"What does it matter? I'll have to leave my friends, my school, my room, my neighborhood . . . everything. I don't want to move."

My father looked at me. "Not quite," he said.

Was your last prediction right? Why or why not?

_____

_____

_____

Make a prediction. What will happen next in the story?

_____

_____

_____

✂ -

My father went on to explain. "We are moving to one of the bigger houses on the other side of the neighborhood. Your grandfather needs some extra help and wants to move in with us. Since we would not have a room for him here, we have decided to move."

"Oh," I said. My emotions felt like they were on a roller coaster. I was thrilled to hear that I'd be able to keep my friends and my school. I did not care about leaving this house for a different house. But now I was worried about my grandfather.

"Your grandfather is okay." My father quickly explained. "He just can't live alone any longer."

I sighed. "Life," I thought. "It is never usual."

Lesson Fourteen

The Writing Assignment

Directions: Write a story that gets readers to make predictions as they read it. Answer the following questions before you begin writing:

1. **How do authors get readers to make predictions?**

   _____

   _____

   _____

   _____

2. **What main events will happen in your story?**

   _____

   _____

   _____

   _____

3. **How will you try to get readers to make predictions as they read your story?**

   _____

   _____

   _____

   _____

The Reading Assignment

Teacher Direction: Evaluate the answers on the reading handout.

Objective	Possible Points	Earned Points
You made predictions as you read.		
You knew whether or not your predictions were right or wrong.		
Total Earned Points:		

The Writing Assignment

Teacher Direction: Evaluate the original stories.

Objective	Possible Points	Earned Points
You wrote an original story that tried to get readers to make predictions as they read.		
You used an imperative sentence in your writing.		
You selected ending punctuation to fit different types of sentences.		
You put effort into the writing process.		
Total Earned Points:		

Additional Teacher Comments: _____

_____

_____

_____

Objectives

Reading

✔ To identify different audiences in similar pieces of writing

Writing

✔ To write for different audiences

✔ To punctuate and use transitions correctly

Lesson Summary

The students will read three different versions of a piece of writing called "The Night Before." Each writing will be about thoughts and feelings of a student the night before the first day of school. However, the audience for each piece of writing will be different. Then, the students will write three versions of an event. Each version of the students' writing will be different because the students will select a different audience for each piece of writing.

Materials Needed

✱ copies of the reading assignment (pages 129–130)

✱ copies of the writing assignment (page 131)

Part I: The Reading Connections

A. Develop interest in the topic.

Ask: "If you wanted to go to the movies with one of your friends, how would you ask your friend if he or she wanted to go with you?" Answers will vary but might include, "Hey, wanna go to the movies?"

Ask: "If you wanted to go to the movies, how would you ask your mother if you could go?" Answers will vary but might include, "Mom, is it okay if I go to the movies with Sara?"

Ask: "If you want to buy tickets to a movie, what would you say to the person at the ticket booth?" Answers will vary but may include, "May I please have a ticket to see a movie?"

Help students recognize the fact that people speak differently when they speak to different people.

B. Encourage students to make predictions about the reading.

Tell the students that they will be reading three pieces of writing called "The Night Before." Although each piece of writing is about the same thing, each piece of writing is written differently.

Ask students to make predictions about what the writings might be about and how the three pieces might be written differently. Encourage students to give creative answers.

Part I: The Reading Connection *(cont.)*

C. Encourage good reading habits.

Teach students that when writers write, they should think about their *audience*. The audience is the people who are going to be reading the writing. By understanding who the audience of a piece of writing is supposed to be, readers can understand why authors choose to write things in different ways.

D. Establish a purpose for reading.

Pass out copies of the three versions of "The Night Before" (pages 129 and 130) for the students to read. Read aloud the instructions that the students should complete as they read the story.

E. Define and extend word meaning.

The word *versions* is used in the instructions. Explain that in movies, books, stories, songs, etc, there are often different versions of the same idea. A *version* is one person's way of looking at something or saying something.

F. Allow ample time for students to read the story and complete the reading assignment.

G. Discuss the answers to the reading assignment together.

* **Version A** was written for the author. The author was very honest with all of her thoughts, and she was just writing things down to help her remember how she was feeling and what she was thinking.

* **Version B** was probably written for a teacher or an adult. Version B was written to explain to someone else what thoughts and feelings students have before the first night of school. The writing is very clear and formal, so anyone could understand it.

* **Version C** was probably written to a friend over e-mail or another computer communication device. It was probably written to a close friend. It was informally written, with grammar errors and incomplete sentences.

Part II: The Writing Connection

A. Develop interest in the topic.

Ask: "When people write, who might their audience be?" Remind the students that the audience is the person reading what was written. Write responses on the board. Possible answers might be bosses, parents, friends, teachers, babysitters, doctors, business associates, workers, children, family members, etc.

Part II: The Writing Connection *(cont.)*

B. Explain the writing assignment to the students.

Explain to the students that they will be writing three different versions of the same event. (Remind students that a version is one way of looking at something or saying something.) Each version will be slightly different because it will be written for a different person.

C. Assist students in organizing their narrative.

Distribute copies of page 131. Help the students gather their ideas. Read aloud the questions on their writing-assignment handout and allow them time to answer each question. Encourage creative thinking.

1. *What event are you going to describe?* Encourage students to think about true events that happened to themselves or to people that they know. Have them think about funny events, scary events, and sad events. Encourage students to make up events, as well, to help generate ideas.

2. *Who is your audience going to be?* Encourage students to select people on the list that was made at the beginning of class or to write to people who were not mentioned on the list.

3. *How might you write differently to each of these three audiences?* Encourage students to think about how they would speak and act differently in front of the different people. Grammar, wording, explanations, and format might change depending on who students were addressing.

D. Allow writing time.

Give students ample time to write their narratives.

E. Give students a strategy to help them revise their writing.

Tell students that when retelling an event, there are some words that can be used to help move the story along from beginning to end. These words are called *transitions*. Some useful transitions for their writing might be *to begin, then, soon, after that, then, suddenly, finally,* and *in the end.* Give students time to revise their work.

F. Give students a strategy to help them edit their writing.

Tell students that a comma is often used after a transition. (*Example:* Later, my friend came into my room.) Give students time to edit, using the new skill.

G. Publish students' ideas.

Pair up the students. Have them read aloud their writing without naming the audience. Have their partner discuss who they think the audience is and why.

The Reading Assignment

Directions: Read the three versions of "The Night Before" below and on page 130. As you read, identify who the audience is for each version.

The Night Before *(Version A)*

Dear Diary,

The first day of school is tomorrow, and I'm a bit nervous and excited. I'm nervous about seeing who's going to be in all of my classes and about meeting all of my new teachers. I hope everyone is nice. I'm excited about seeing all of my friends again. I didn't get to see most of them over the summer. Oh, well. We'll see how it goes. At least I have a cute new outfit to wear. I hope no one else wears the same shirt as me. Anyway, guess I should go to bed. I'll let you know what happen . . .

Who was the audience? How do you know? _____

_____

_____

_____

_____

Lesson
Fifteen

The Reading Assignment *(cont.)*

The Night Before *(Version B)*

The night before school starts brings many different feelings. Some students become nervous about meeting new people. They hope that they will have friends in their classes. Also, students are nervous about meeting their new teachers. They hope their teachers will get along with them. They also hope that their teachers will be able to teach them many new things.

Students also are excited about school starting. They are excited to see all the friends that they have not seen over the summer. They are also excited about talking about their summers and hearing about other people's summers.

Many students get ready for the first day of school by picking out the "right" outfit to wear. Students also spend time organizing themselves for the new year ahead.

Who was the audience? How do you know? _____

_____

_____

_____

_____

The Night Before *(Version C)*

hey kate. schools starts tomorrow. i have a new outfit to wear. hope i like the other kids in the class. hope the teachers are cool. what are you wearing? do you know who is in your class? got to log off now. my brother needs the computer.

Who was the audience? How do you know? _____

_____

_____

_____

_____

The Writing Assignment

Directions: Write about one event in three different ways. Each piece of writing should be a little different because the audience for the writing should be different. Before writing, answer the questions below.

> **Remember, the *audience* of a piece of writing is the people who are going to be reading it.**

1. **What event are you going to describe?** _____

   _____

   _____

   _____

2. **Who is your audience going to be for each of your three different versions? (Make sure you have a different audience for each version.)**

   Version 1: _____

   Version 2: _____

   Version 3: _____

3. **How might you write differently to each of these three audiences?**

   _____

   _____

   _____

   _____

   _____

   _____

   _____

The Reading Assignment

Teacher Direction: Evaluate the answers on the reading handout.

Objective	Possible Points	Earned Points
You figured out the audience in different pieces of writing.		
You explained how you figured out who the audience was.		
Total Earned Points:		

The Writing Connection

Teacher Direction: Evaluate the different versions of the stories.

Objective	Possible Points	Earned Points
You picked different audiences for your writing.		
You wrote differently depending on who your audience was.		
You punctuated and used transitions in your writing.		
You put effort into the writing process.		
Total Earned Points:		

Additional Teacher Comments: _____

_____

_____

_____

_____

National Standard Correlations

Listed below are the McREL standards for Language Arts Level 2 (Grades 3–5). All standards and benchmarks are used with permission from McREL.

Copyright 2004 McREL

Mid-continent Research for Education and Learning

2550 S. Parker Road, Suite 500

Aurora, CO 80014

Telephone: (303) 337-0990

Website: *www.mcrel.org/standards-benchmarks*

McREL Standards are in **bold.** Benchmarks are in regular print. The correlating lessons that meet each objective are in *italics.*

Standard 1: Uses the general skills and strategies of the writing process.

1. Prewriting: Uses prewriting strategies to plan written work (e.g., uses graphic organizers, story maps, and webs; groups related ideas; takes notes; brainstorms ideas; organizes information according to type and purpose of writing)

✦ *Lesson One*	✦ *Lesson Six*	✦ *Lesson Eleven*
✦ *Lesson Two*	✦ *Lesson Seven*	✦ *Lesson Thirteen*
✦ *Lesson Three*	✦ *Lesson Eight*	✦ *Lesson Fourteen*
✦ *Lesson Four*	✦ *Lesson Nine*	✦ *Lesson Fifteen*
✦ *Lesson Five*	✦ *Lesson Ten*	

2. Drafting and Revising: Uses prewriting strategies to draft and revise written work (e.g., eleborates on a central ideas; writes with attention to audience, word choice, sentence variation; uses paragraphs to develop separate ideas; produces multiple drafts)

✦ *Lesson Two*	✦ *Lesson Nine*	✦ *Lesson Thirteen*
✦ *Lesson Four*	✦ *Lesson Ten*	✦ *Lesson Fourteen*
✦ *Lesson Seven*	✦ *Lesson Eleven*	✦ *Lesson Fifteen*
✦ *Lesson Eight*	✦ *Lesson Twelve*	

Standard 1 *(cont.)*

3. Editing and Publishing: Uses strategies to edit and publish written work (e.g., edits for grammar, punctuation, capitalization, and spelling at a developmentally appropriate level; uses reference materials; considers page format [paragraphs, margins, indentations, titles]; selects presentation format according to purpose; incorporates photos, illustrations, charts, and graphs; uses available technology to compose and publish work)

   + *Lesson One*   + *Lesson Five*   + *Lesson Twelve*

   + *Lesson Two*   + *Lesson Seven*   + *Lesson Thirteen*

   + *Lesson Three*   + *Lesson Ten*   + *Lesson Fourteen*

   + *Lesson Four*   + *Lesson Eleven*   + *Lesson Fifteen*

4. Evaluates own and others' writing: (e.g., determines the best feature of a piece of writing, determines how own writing achieves its purposes, asks for feedback, responds to classmates' writing)

   + *Lesson Five*   + *Lesson Seven*   + *Lesson Thirteen*

   + *Lesson Six*   + *Lesson Eight*   + *Lesson Fourteen*

5. Uses strategies: (e.g., adapts focus, organization, point of view; determines knowledge and interests of audience) to write for different audiences (e.g., self, peers, teachers, adults)

   + *Lesson Eight*   + *Lesson Fifteen*

6. Uses strategies: (e.g., adapts focus, point of view, organization, form) to write for a variety of purposes (e.g., to inform, entertain, explain, describe, record ideas)

   + *Lesson One*   + *Lesson Five*   + *Lesson Ten*

   + *Lesson Two*   + *Lesson Six*   + *Lesson Twelve*

   + *Lesson Four*   + *Lesson Nine*   + *Lesson Thirteen*

Standard 1 *(cont.)*

7. Writes expository compositions: (e.g., identifies and stays on the topic; develops the topic with simple facts, details, examples, and explanations; excludes extraneous and inappropriate information; uses structures such as cause-and effect, chronology, similarities and differences; uses several sources of information; provides a concluding statement)

   - ✦ *Lesson Eight*
   - ✦ *Lesson Twelve*

8. Writing narrative accounts, such as poems and stories: (e.g., establishes a context that enables the reader to imagine the event or experience; develops characters, setting, and plot; creates an organizing structure; sequences events; uses concrete sensory details; uses strategies such as dialogue, tension, and suspense; uses an identifiable voice)

   - ✦ *Lesson Two*
   - ✦ *Lesson Seven*
   - ✦ *Lesson Eleven*
   - ✦ *Lesson Three*
   - ✦ *Lesson Eight*
   - ✦ *Lesson Fourteen*
   - ✦ *Lesson Four*
   - ✦ *Lesson Ten*

9. Writing autobiographical compositions: (e.g., provides a context within which the incident occurs, uses simple narrative strategies, and provides some insight into why this incident is memorable)

   - ✦ *Lesson Seven*

10. Writes expressive compositions: (e.g., expresses ideas, reflections, and observations; uses an individual, authentic voice; uses narrative strategies, relevant details, and ideas that enable the reader to imagine the world of the event or experience)

    - ✦ *Lesson One*
    - ✦ *Lesson Seven*
    - ✦ *Lesson Eleven*
    - ✦ *Lesson Three*

11. Writes in response to literature: (e.g., summarizes main ideas and significant details; relates own ideas to supporting details; advances judgments; supports judgments with references to the text, other authors, nonprint media, and personal knowledge)

    - ✦ *Lesson Four*
    - ✦ *Lesson Ten*
    - ✦ *Lesson Fourteen*
    - ✦ *Lesson Six*

12. Writes personal letters: (e.g., includes the date, address, greeting, body, and closing; addresses envelopes; includes signature)

    - ✦ *Lesson Six*
    - ✦ *Lesson Eight*

Standard 2: Uses the stylistic and rhetorical aspects of writing

1. Uses descriptive language that clarifies and enchances ideas: (e.g., common figure of speech, sensory details)

   ✦ *Lesson Two*   ✦ *Lesson Nine*   ✦ *Lesson Ten*

   ✦ *Lesson Four*

2. Uses paragraph form in writing: (e.g., includes the first word of a pargraph, uses topic sentences, recognizes a paragraph as a group of sentences about one main idea, uses an introductory and concluding paragraph, writes several related paragraphs)

   ✦ *Lesson Two*   ✦ *Lesson Ten*   ✦ *Lesson Thirteen*

3. Uses a variety of sentence structures in writing: (e.g., expands basic sentence patterns, uses exclamatory and imperative sentences)

   ✦ *Lesson Seven*   ✦ *Lesson Ten*   ✦ *Lesson Fourteen*

   ✦ *Lesson Nine*

Standard 3: Uses grammatical and mechanical conventions in written compositions

1. Writes in cursive

2. Uses pronouns in written compositions (e.g., substitutes pronouns for nouns, uses pronoun agreement)

3. Uses nouns in written compositions (e.g., uses plural and singular naming words, forms regular and irregular plurals of nouns, uses common and proper nouns, uses nouns as subjects)

4. Uses verbs in written compositions (e.g., uses a wide variety of action verbs, past and present verb tenses, simple tenses, forms of regular verbs, verbs that agree with the subject)

5. Uses adjectives in written compositions (e.g., indefinite, numerical, predicate adjectives)

6. Uses adverbs in written compositions (e.g., to make comparisons)

   ✦ *Lesson Three*

7. Uses coordinating conjunctions in written compositions (e.g., links ideas using connecting words)

   ✦ *Lesson Seven*

Standard 3: Uses grammatical and mechanical conventions in written compositions (cont.)

8. Uses negatives in written compositions (e.g., avoids double negatives)

9. Uses conventions of spelling in written compositions (e.g., spells high frequency, commonly mispelled words from appropriate grade-level list; uses a dictionary and other resources to spell words; uses initial consonant substitution to spell related words; uses vowel combinations for correct spelling; uses contractions, compounds, roots, suffixes, and syllables constructions to spell words)

   ✦ *Lesson Twelve*

10. Uses conventions of capitalization in written compositions (e.g., titles of people; proper nouns [names of towns, cities, counties, and states; days of the week; months of the year; names of streets; names of counties; holidays]; first word of direct quotations; heading, salutation, and closing of a letters)

    ✦ *Lesson One*   ✦ *Lesson Eleven*

11. Uses conventions of punctuation in written compositions (e.g., uses periods after imperative sentences and in initials, abbreviations, and titles before names; uses commas in dates and addresses and after greetings and closings in a letter; uses apostrophes in contractions and possessive nouns; uses quotation marks around titles and with direct quotations; uses a colon between hour and minutes)

    ✦ *Lesson Three*   ✦ *Lesson Eight*   ✦ *Lesson Fourteen*
    ✦ *Lesson Five*

Standard 4: Gathers and uses information for research purposes

1. Uses a variety of strategies to plan research (e.g., identifies possible topic by brainstorming, listing questions, using idea webs; organizes prior knowledge about a topic; develops a course of action; determines how to locate necessary information)

   ✦ *Lesson One*   ✦ *Lesson Five*

2. Uses encyclopedias to gather information for research topics

3. Uses dictionaries to gather information for research topics

---

Standard 4: Gathers and uses information for research purposes *(cont.)*

4. Uses electronic media to gather information (e.g., databases, Internet, CD-ROM, television shows, cassette recordings, videos, pull-down menus, word searches)

5. Uses key words, guide words, alphabetical and numerical order, indexes, cross-references, and letters on volumes to find information for research topics

   ✦ *Lesson Five*

6. Uses multiple representations of information (e.g., maps, charts, photos, diagrams, tables) to find information for research topics

7. Uses strategies to gather and record information for research topics (e.g., uses notes, maps, charts, graphs, tables, and other graphic organizers; paraphrases and summarizes information; gathers direct quotes; provides narrative descriptions)

   ✦ *Lesson One*   ✦ *Lesson Five*

8. Uses strategies to compile information into written reports or summaries (e.g., incorporates notes into a finished product; includes simple facts, details, explanations, and examples; draws conclusions from relationships and patterns that emerge from data from different sources; uses appropriate visual aids and media)

   ✦ *Lesson One*

9. Cites information sources (e.g., quotes or paraphrases information sources, lists resources used by title)

   ✦ *Lesson Five*

Standard 5: Uses the general skills and strategies of the reading process

1. Previews text (e.g., skims material; uses pictures, textual clues, and text format)

2. Establishes a purpose for reading (e.g., for information, for pleasure, to understand a specific viewpoint)

   ✦ *Lesson Four*   ✦ *Lesson Six*

National Standard Correlations (cont.)

Standard 5 *(cont.)*

3. Makes, confirms, and revises simple predictions about what will be found in a text (e.g., uses prior knowledge and ideas presented in text, illustrations, titles, topic sentences, key words, and foreshadowing clues)

   - ✦ *Lesson One*
   - ✦ *Lesson Two*
   - ✦ *Lesson Three*
   - ✦ *Lesson Four*
   - ✦ *Lesson Five*
   - ✦ *Lesson Six*
   - ✦ *Lesson Seven*
   - ✦ *Lesson Eight*
   - ✦ *Lesson Nine*
   - ✦ *Lesson Ten*
   - ✦ *Lesson Eleven*
   - ✦ *Lesson Thirteen*
   - ✦ *Lesson Fourteen*
   - ✦ *Lesson Fifteen*

4. Uses phonetic and structural analysis techniques, syntactic structure, and semantic context to decode unknown words (e.g., vowel patterns, complex word families, syllabication, root words, affixes)

   - ✦ *Lesson One*
   - ✦ *Lesson Two*
   - ✦ *Lesson Five*
   - ✦ *Lesson Eight*
   - ✦ *Lesson Eleven*
   - ✦ *Lesson Twelve*

5. Uses a variety of context clues to decode unknown words (e.g., draws on earlier reading, reads ahead)

6. Uses word reference materials (e.g., glossary, dictionary, thesaurus) to determine the meaning, pronunciation, and derivations of unknown words

7. Understands level-appropriate reading vocabulary (e.g., synonyms, antonyms, homophones, multi-meaning words)

8. Monitors own reading strategies and makes modifications as needed (e.g., recognizes when he or she is confused by a section of text, questions whether the text makes sense)

   - ✦ *Lesson Thirteen*

9. Adjusts speed of reading to suit purpose and difficulty of the material

   - ✦ *Lesson Thirteen*

10. Understands the author's purpose (e.g., to persuade, to inform) or point of view

    - ✦ *Lesson Six*

11. Uses personal criteria to select reading material (e.g., personal interest, knowledge of authors and genres, text difficulty, recommendations of others)

> **Standard 6: Uses reading skills and strategies to understand and interpret a variety of literary texts**

1. Uses reading skills and strategies to understand a variety of literary passages and texts (e.g., fairy tales, folktales, fiction, nonfiction, myths, poems, fables, fantasies, historical fiction, biographies, autobiographies, chapter books)

   ✦ *Lesson One*   ✦ *Lesson Three*   ✦ *Lesson Four*

   ✦ *Lesson Two*

2. Knows the defining characteristics of a variety of literary forms and genres (e.g., fairy tales, folk tales, fiction, nonfiction, myths, poems, fables, fantasies, historical fiction, biographies, autobiographies, chapter books)

   ✦ *Lesson One*   ✦ *Lesson Three*   ✦ *Lesson Four*

   ✦ *Lesson Two*

3. Understands the basic concept of plot (e.g., main problem, conflict, resolution, cause-and-effect)

   ✦ *Lesson Four*   ✦ *Lesson Eleven*

4. Understands similarities and differences within and among literary works from various genre and cultures (e.g., in terms of settings, character types, events, point of view; role of natural phenomena)

5. Understands elements of character development in literary works (e.g., differences between main and minor characters; stereotypical characters as opposed to fully-developed characters; changes that characters undergo; the importance of a character's actions, motives, and appearance to plot and theme)

   ✦ *Lesson Four*   ✦ *Lesson Ten*

6. Knows themes that recur across literary works

7. Understands the ways in which language is used in literary texts (e.g., personification, alliteration, onomatopoeia, simile, metaphor, imagery, hyperbole, beat, rhythm)

   ✦ *Lesson Nine*

8. Makes connections between characters or simple events in a literary work and people or events in his or her own life

   ✦ *Lesson Seven*   ✦ *Lesson Ten*

Standard 7: Uses reading skills and strategies to understand and interpret a variety of informational texts

1. Uses reading skills and strategies to understand a variety of informational texts (e.g., textbooks, biographical sketches, letters, diaries, directions, procedures, magazines)

   ✦ *Lesson One*   ✦ *Lesson Twelve*   ✦ *Lesson Thirteen*

2. Knows the defining characteristics of a variety of informational texts (e.g., textbooks, biographical sketches, letters, diaries, directions, procedures, magazines)

   ✦ *Lesson One*   ✦ *Lesson Six*

3. Uses text organizers (e.g., headings, topic and summary sentences, graphic features, typeface, chapter titles) to determine the main ideas and to locate information in a text

4. Uses the various parts of a book (e.g., index, table of contents, glossary, appendix, preface) to locate information

5. Summarizes and paraphrases information in texts (e.g., includes the main idea and significant supporting details of a reading selection)

   ✦ *Lesson Five*

6. Uses prior knowledge and experience to understand and respond to new information

7. Understands structural patterns or organization in informational texts (e.g., chronological, logical, or sequential order; compare-and-contrast; cause-and-effect; proposition and support)

   ✦ *Lesson Eight*   ✦ *Lesson Twelve*

Standard 8: Uses listening and speaking strategies for different purposes

1. Contributes to group discussions.

2. Asks questions in class (e.g., when he or she is confused, to seek others' opinions, responds)

3. Responds to questions and comments (e.g., gives reasons in support of opinions, responds to others' ideas)

   ✦ *Lesson Fourteen*

4. Listens to classmates and adults (e.g., does not interrup, faces the speaker, asks questions, summarizes or paraphrases to confirm understanding, gives feedback, elimates barriers to effective listening)

   ✦ *Lesson One*   ✦ *Lesson Eight*   ✦ *Lesson Fourteen*

Standard 8 (cont.)

5. Uses strategies to convey a clear main point when speaking (e.g., expresses ideas in a logical manner, uses specific vocabulary to establish tone and present information)

6. Uses level-appropriate vocabulary in speech (e.g., familiar idioms, similes, word play)

7. Makes basic oral presentations to class (e.g., uses subject-related information and vocabulary; includes content appropriate to the audience; relates ideas and observations; incorporates visual aids or props; incorporates several sources of information)

8. Uses a variety of nonverbal communication skills (e.g., eye contact, gestures, facial expressions, posture)

9. Uses a variety of verbal communication skills (e.g., projection, tone, volume, rate, articulation, pace, phrasing)

   ✦ *Lesson Eight*

10. Organizes ideas for oral presentations (e.g., uses an introduction and conclusion; uses notes or other memory aids; organizes ideas around major points, in sequence, or chronologically; uses traditional structures, such as cause-and-effect, similarity and difference, posing and answering a question; uses details, examples, and anecdotes to clarify information)

11. Listens for specific information in spoken texts (e.g., plot details or information about a character in a short story read aloud, information about a familiar topic from a radio broadcast)

12. Understands the main ideas and supporting details in spoken texts (e.g., presentations by peers or quest speakers, a current affairs report on the radio)

13. Listens to and understands persuasive messages (e.g., television commercials, commands and requests, pressure from peers)

14. Interprets the use of nonverbal cues used in conversation

15. Knows specific ways in which language is used in real-life situations (e.g., buying something from a shopkeeper, requesting something from a parent, arguing with a sibling, talking to a friend)

16. Understands that language reflects different regions and cultures (e.g., sayings; expressions; usage; oral traditions and customs; historical, geographical, and societal influences on language)

References

Lesson One: Biographies

Amet, Phil. "Chester Greenwood." Troy MI: 1997–2005. The Great Idea Finder. March, 2005. (4 March, 2005)

Lesson Two: Fairy Tales

"Fairy Tales from Life." IRA/NCTE. Feb. 9, 2005. (10 Feb. 2005)

http://www.readwritethink.org/lessons/lesson_view.asp?id=42

Lesson Three: Fables

"Fable." Turner Learning, Inc. 1999. (8 Feb. 2005)

http://www.turnerlearning.com/tntlearning/animalfarm/affable.html

Cook, Kathy. "Elements of Fables." ArtsEdge and the John F. Kennedy Center for the Performing Arts. (7 Feb. 2005)

http://artsedge.kennedy-center.org/content/2221/

Lesson Four: Myths

Cook, Kathy. "Elements of Myths." ArtsEdge and the John F. Kennedy Center for the Performing Arts. (9 Feb. 2005)

http://artsedge.kennedy-center.org/content/2232/

Park, James and Corbett, Sally. "An Introduction to Ancient Greece: Greek and Roman Goddesses and Gods." Highland Park Elementary School. 1997. (9 Feb. 2005)

http://www.hipark.austin.isd.tenet.edu/mythology/gkgods_heroes.html>

"African Gods and Their Associates." Untagle Incorporated. June 26, 2002. (9 Feb. 2005)

http://www.mythome.org/africang.html>

"Names of Gods and Goddesses." Chinaroads. May 2003. (9 Feb. 2005)

http://www.lowchensaustralia.com/names/gods.htm>

Lesson Five: Researching Skills

"Create an MLA Works Cited Page." The Writing Center: University of Wisconsin-Madison. 2004. (18 Feb. 2005)

http://www.wisc.edu/writing/Handbook/DocMLA.html

Lesson Eight: Organizational Patterns in Reading and Writing

"Format for a Friendly or Personal Letter." English Plus. 1997–2001. (19 Feb. 2005)

http://englishplus.com/grammar/00000144.htm>

References

Lesson Nine: Literary Language

Ware, Robert. OneLook Dictionary Search. "Poetry." 1996. (6 March 2005)

   http://www.onelook.com/>

Lesson Eleven: Understanding Plot

Spears, Deanne. "Improving Reading Skills, 4/e & Developing Critical Reading Skills, 5/e." Student Resourced: Latin Roots. McGraw Hill. 2000. (2 July 2005)

   http://www.mhhe.com/socscience/english/spears/stu3/studisk/word_parts_lists/latinroots.htm.

Lesson Twelve: Examining Informational Patterns in Textbooks

Levenson, George. "How to Grow Pumpkins." Pumpkin Circle. 1998–2004. (2 July 2005)

   http://www.sadako.com/pumpkin/growing.html.

University of Illinois Extension. "Pumpkins and More." Urban Programs Resource Network. (3 July 2005)

   http://www.urbanext.uiuc.edu/pumpkins/varieties.html

Lesson Fourteen: Making Predictions

Harper, Douglas. Online Etymology Dictionary. "Prediction." 2001. (4 April 2005)

   http://www.etymonline.com/index.php?search=prediction&searchmode=none

Spalding, Cathy. About. "Types of Sentences." 2005. (19 July 2005)

   http://homeworktips.about.com/cs/grammar/a/sentences.htm

National Standard Correlations

McREL: Mid-Continent Research for Education and Learning. Content Knowledge (4th Edition). 2004. (14 Feb. 2005)

   http://www.mcrel.org/compendium/browse.asp